UNLEASHING THE POTENTIAL OF THE SMALLER CHURCH

edited by SHAWN MCMULLEN

UNLEASHING THE POTENTIAL OF THE SMALLER CHURCH

edited by SHAWN MCMULLEN

VISION

AND

STRATEGY

FOR

LIFE-CHANGING

MINISTRY

Cover design by Rule 29
Inside design by Anita Cook

Library of Congress Cataloging-in-Publication Data

Unleashing the potential of the smaller church : vision and strategy for life-changing ministry / edited by Shawn McMullen.
    p. cm.
 ISBN 0-7847-1621-8 (pbk.)
 1. Small churches. I. McMullen, Shawn A.

BV637.8.U55 2006
253--dc22

                                                2006002184

Standard Publishing, Cincinnati, Ohio. A division of Standex International Corporation. © 2006 by Standard Publishing. All rights reserved. Printed in the United States of America.

12 11 10 09 08 07 06   7 6 5 4 3 2 1

ISBN 0-7847-1621-8

DEDICATIONS

*To my father and mother, Wilbur and Margaret McMullen,
who for more than 60 years cheerfully devoted their marriage,
their time, their resources, and their family in service to the smaller
church. "Whatever you do, work at it with all your heart,
as working for the Lord, not for men, since you know that you
will receive an inheritance from the Lord as a reward.
It is the Lord Christ you are serving" (Colossians 3:23, 24).*

*To the faithful men and women who love, serve,
and support smaller churches everywhere. "Therefore,
my dear brothers [and sisters], stand firm. Let nothing move you.
Always give yourselves fully to the work of the Lord, because
you know that your labor in the Lord is not in vain"
(1 Corinthians 15:58).*

You're making a difference. Thank you.

TABLE OF CONTENTS

FOREWORD

by Bob Russell, Minister
Southeast Christian Church
Louisville, Kentucky

Pardon me for bragging, but I'm really proud of the American church these days. In recent years the world has accused the church of being unloving and hypocritical. Even some within the church have attacked it as being totally irrelevant and out-of-touch.

But after Hurricane Katrina left hundreds of thousands in the Gulf Coast in desperate circumstances, guess who responded with the most generous and most practical help? The church. The day after the hurricane ravaged the area, hundreds of churches, big and small, responded with much-needed assistance.

While government and relief agencies faltered, churches housed displaced citizens in makeshift shelters, channeled food and water to needy families, raised money for immediate help, and developed strategies for long-term assistance.

This outpouring of compassion to the needy has been wonderful to witness, and it has given a measure of much-needed credibility to the church. But the danger of this renewed benevolence emphasis is that we could lose our primary focus, which is evangelism. Jesus' commission to us is still to "go and make disciples of all nations, baptizing them in the name of the Father and of the Son and of the Holy Spirit, and teaching them to obey everything I have commanded you" (Matthew 28:19, 20).

The world applauds the benevolent church because their efforts are tangible and compassionate. But evangelism often makes people uncomfortable since it confronts the need to repent of sin and requires surrender to the Lordship of Christ. From the day Paul frightened Felix with his discourse on righteousness, self-control, and the judgment to come, evangelism seems intolerant, pushy, and impractical.

That's why I'm most encouraged by those churches that maintain a healthy balance. They care for the needy, but evangelism continues to be the main thing. Some remarkable things are happening in those kinds of churches all across America. They are fulfilling Jesus' commission without apology. They speak the truth in love and are making a dramatic difference in people's lives and in their communities.

While the growth of megachurches has received a lot of attention, there are hundreds of smaller congregations that are not as well publicized but are coming alive and making a huge difference in their communities.

In his book, *Unleashing the Potential of the Smaller Church*, Shawn McMullen does an excellent job of sharing examples and ideas of how congregations of less than 200 in attendance can transform lives and significantly impact their neighborhoods for Christ. The testimonies from more than a dozen dynamic ministries in a variety of situations will inspire any who are involved in a smaller congregation with a "can-do" mentality.

This material will help motivate church leaders to lift their vision and increase their church's impact on their community. The Lord's promise in Ephesians 3:20, 21 applies to the smaller church as well as the larger one: "Now to him who is able to do immeasurably more than all we ask or imagine, according to his power that is at work within us, to him be glory in the church and in Christ Jesus throughout all generations, for ever and ever! Amen."

FOREWORD

by Rick Atchley, Minister
Richland Hills Church of Christ
North Richland Hills, Texas

Solomon said, "Of the making of books there is no end." There is no shortage of new books to read. There is a shortage, however, of new books worth reading. This is one of those books.

There are several reasons why I am delighted to endorse this work. First, it is another example of the worth and witness of pursuing unity. I am excited to see more and more church leaders unite around the mission of Jesus to reach the lost. We can be so much more fruitful together than we can be apart.

Second, this is a book about the church, and I am a strong believer in the primacy of the church as Jesus' chosen agency for accomplishing his agenda on earth. The writers in this book have given their lives to build up Jesus' church. They love the church, believe in the church, and will not settle for anything less than the church at her very best. Neither will Jesus. Neither should we.

Finally, I am excited to see a book that celebrates the value and importance of the smaller church. What a debt the kingdom owes to faithful servants of smaller churches! What a debt I owe! I came to faith in a small church. I was loved right into the kingdom by men and women in that little church. It was in their midst that I put on Christ in baptism, prayed my first public prayer, and preached my first sermon. I cherish many sweet memories of those days.

However, some of my memories are bittersweet, for the church that raised me no longer exists. The culture around it changed, and the congregation refused to embrace that change for the sake of the gospel. It brings me great sadness to think that a once vibrant body of Christ has lost its witness in a community that desperately needs Jesus. Too often this is how the last chapters read in the stories of many smaller churches. But it does not have to be this way! We do believe in a God of revival, don't we?

In this book you will read about smaller churches where God is alive, where the kingdom is expanding, where lives are being changed. You will be reminded that God is not looking at the size of the auditorium, but the size of the hearts of the people who worship in it. And you will be reminded that the gates of Hell cannot prevail against the church of Jesus!

So read on, be blessed, and dream big!

ACKNOWLEDGEMENTS

By its nature this book is a collaborative effort. I'm thankful for the thirteen contributors from across the country who helped make it a reality.

I owe a special debt of gratitude to Sheryl Overstreet, administrative assistant for THE LOOKOUT. As the manuscripts came in for this project, Sheryl volunteered (on her own time) to format the material and enter corrections. She not only did her work carefully and thoroughly, she did it willingly and cheerfully.

I'm grateful to my friend and fellow editor Mark Taylor, who encouraged me at every stage of this project. Mark's thoughtful insights and timely advice have been invaluable.

I'm grateful to my spiritual family, the Church of Christ in Milan, Indiana, for the warm relationships and positive experiences we've shared together the past six years—relationships and experiences that set the stage for this book. Their patience with my schedule and their willingness to work around my role as editor of THE LOOKOUT make my ministry with them a joy. I'm honored to be their preacher.

Finally, I'm grateful for the support and encouragement of my wonderful wife and partner, Ree—not only in this writing project but in all I do. Her patience and her willingness to give up some of our time together as I completed this book are gifts I do not take lightly.

A NOTE FROM THE EDITOR

I grew up in a smaller church. As I recall, most years our annual average worship attendance ran somewhere between 150 and 175. Some years that figure was considerably less.

We weren't a large congregation by most standards, but God did some great things in our midst. We had a dynamic youth group (several members of this group went on to prepare for ministry), a vibrant youth choir (we sang in local churches and toured for one week every summer), and a competitive Bible Bowl team (we placed among the top 16 teams in the nation the summer before my senior year in high school).

Then there were the relationships. I knew every elder and deacon in our church, every Sunday school teacher, every youth worker. I knew every child and senior adult in our congregation.

My home church challenged me to develop teaching and leadership skills. I was in junior high school when I began assisting in junior church and helping with Vacation Bible School. During my high school years I sang in the adult choir, helped served Communion and collect the weekly offering, and preached occasionally on Sunday evenings. I was encouraged in everything I attempted.

I was ordained into the Christian ministry at this church—along with three of my closest friends. Our multiple ordination service drew a great crowd, including a reporter from our local newspaper. Our photographs, along with a newspaper article covering the ordination service, are still proudly displayed on a wall in the church foyer.

I owe much to my home church. And I'm just one member of one family. Thinking about the hundreds—even thousands—of lives this congregation has affected through the years helps me understand the far-reaching impact this smaller church has had on the kingdom. It has produced missionaries, Bible college professors, preachers, teachers, musicians, youth workers, and simply good, solid, dependable Christian families.

Outside of what I've written, you may never hear much about my home church. But I don't think anyone at the church minds. The good folks of this good church have been content for generations simply to do God's work the best way they know how.

Someday, when we all get to Heaven, we'll know more about the impact of this smaller church in God's eternal plan. Until then, they will continue faithfully and effectively to do what they've always done: make disciples, one person at a time.

Does my story sound familiar? Have you had a similar experience in a smaller church? Whether you have or you haven't, I think you'll find this book enlightening, encouraging, and motivating. It's all about smaller churches and the great things they are doing for Christ. I hope you're challenged by it.

—Shawn McMullen

CHAPTER ONE

THE KIDDERMINSTER PRINCIPLE

SHAWN MCMULLEN

I AM THE MINISTER OF THE CHURCH OF CHRIST IN MILAN, INDIANA. Milan is a small, semirural community (population 1,816) nestled in the eastern edge of Ripley County. Our little town is famous, although you might not have known it. In 1954, Milan's tiny high school (161 students) sent a team to the Indiana state high school basketball tournament to take on powerhouse Muncie Central. Milan won the state title with a heart-stopping last second shot by guard Bobby Plump. *Sports Illustrated* listed this team among the top twenty teams of the twentieth century. Indiana sports writers named this the No. 1 sports story in Indiana history. The team's success (they are the smallest team in history to win the state title) inspired the beloved basketball movie Hoosiers.

It's hard to miss the moral of the story: you don't have to be big to be good.

That's true of churches too. And it's a good thing, because predominantly we're a nation of smaller churches.

A recent study released by Barna Research[1] reported that the typical church in America has an average worship attendance of eighty-nine adults—that a full 60 percent of Protestant churches in our country are attended by one hundred or fewer adults in worship. In fact, only 12 percent of American adults attend churches of one thousand or more adults.

This is not to downplay the significance of larger churches. They're here to stay, and they play a vital role in the work of God's kingdom. I thank God for larger churches and for those who lead and serve in them.

Still, smaller churches (I'm referring to churches with an average Sunday worship attendance of two hundred or less) are in the majority in our country, and they are crucial to the advancement of God's kingdom on earth. Barna observed,

> Small churches play an important and valuable role in the religious landscape of America. They reach millions of young adults who have no interest in a larger church setting. They have tremendous potential for

building strong community, as well as spiritual foundations. And smaller churches often grow into larger churches once they develop significant internal leadership and creatively overcome their resource limitations.[2]

If you're part of a smaller church, you're part of something very, very big.

Why You Should Read This Book

You need to read this book if:

- You're a member of a smaller church.
- You're a leader or volunteer in a smaller church.
- You're struggling with your ministry in a smaller church.
- You want your smaller church to make a difference in your community.

You also need to read this book if:

- You're a member of a smaller church and you're satisfied with the ministry God has given you.
- You're a member of a smaller church and you would like to learn about and celebrate God's work in other smaller churches.

What You'll Gain by Reading It

Proverbs 16:3 says, "Commit to the LORD whatever you do, and your plans will succeed."

I can't promise you this book will change the course of your ministry or multiply your church's impact on its community. After all, it's only a book—a little ink and a little paper. But if you'll give it a thoughtful reading, pay attention to the advice and action steps found in each chapter, and prayerfully commit your plans to the Lord, I believe you and your congregation will see good things happen as God works out his divine purpose in your life, your congregation, and your community.

Having said that, here are a few things I believe you'll be able to take away from this book:

- A renewed self-image as a leader or volunteer in your church
- A plan for renewing the self-image of your congregation as a whole
- A clearer sense of your church's value, mission, and purpose
- A plan of action to motivate your people to ministry and multiply your church's impact in your community

- A view of your church as a vital part of a large network of Christian workers who are collectively making a difference for Christ in this world

Are you with me? Let's get started!

The Kidderminster Principle

Richard Baxter was a Puritan. Born in London in 1615, Baxter entered the ministry at the age of twenty-six. He spent his early ministry years as an army chaplain, and the next fourteen years (1647–1661) ministering with a church in Kidderminster, Worcestershire, England. He had a passion for preaching. (He's well known for his maxim, "I preached as never sure to preach again; and as a dying man to dying men.") He also had a passion for souls—every soul in his community, in fact.

Kidderminster was a notoriously corrupt community, and Baxter had his work cut out for him. Nevertheless, this small community was dramatically transformed during Baxter's ministry.

In an article titled "Prayer Makes History," writer David Smithers notes, "When Baxter arrived in Kidderminster it had a population of about 3,000 weavers who were reckless, ungodly, and content to remain that way. By the end of Baxter's stay, the entire community was miraculously transformed by the power of the Holy Spirit.[3]

Writer Leonard Ravenhill observed,

> The outcome of this contagious passion is best measured by Baxter's own words: "To the praise of my gracious Master . . . the church at Kidderminster became so full on the Lord's Day that we had to build galleries to contain all the people. Our weekday meetings also were always full. On the Lord's Day all disorder became quite banished out of the town. As you passed along the streets on the Sabbath morning, you might hear a hundred households singing psalms at their family worship. In a word, when I came to Kidderminster, there was only about one family in a whole street that worshipped God and called upon His name. When I left, there were some streets where not a family did not do so. And though we had 600 communicants, there were not twelve in whose salvation I had not perfect confidence."[4]

Ravenhill adds, "As one writer expresses with beauty, 'Through his preaching and the power of his holy life, the whole community was changed from a habitation of cruelty and immorality to a garden of true piety.'"[5]

What does the ministry of a seventeenth-century Puritan preacher have to do with you? Let me put it this way: if you're part of a smaller church in America, it has everything to do with you! A simple principle couched in Baxter's story has the potential to revolutionize your ministry, the church you serve, and the community where you live.

Based on Baxter's successful ministry in a small community, I call it the Kidderminster Principle, and it goes like this: *Regardless of the location or size of your church, you have the potential to engage in life-changing ministry that transforms your community*. You don't need to relocate. You don't need an advanced degree in church growth. You don't need additional staff. With God's help, you can begin right where you are and make an eternal difference.

A Matter of Perspective

But let's back up for a moment. This is not a shallow pep talk for discouraged church leaders and volunteers. This book is designed to challenge you to do something you may never have considered—to stay where you are, commit to a long-term ministry, learn from others who have done the same, and impact your church and community for the cause of Christ.

I serve a smaller church in a small community. I also speak frequently in other churches, many of them smaller congregations. So if you're serving a smaller church, I know right where you're coming from.

Not long ago I held an evangelistic meeting for a smaller church in a small Midwestern community. I spent several days with the preacher and his family. As we went about our work that week, I was amazed at how well this preacher knew the people in his town. When we sat on his front porch, people strolling by stopped and talked, usually expressing their appreciation to the preacher for his counsel or encouragement during a difficult time. When we walked into a nearby diner for breakfast, the preacher stopped at every table (I'm not exaggerating!) and spoke to someone he knew.

This man was having a profound impact on the people in his community. But when we sat on his front porch in the quiet of the evening, he talked about the discouragement he felt in his ministry. Many of his seminary classmates had gone on to serve larger congregations, and this made him feel as if he had failed. I sensed a similar feeling among some members of the congregation.

For lack of a better phrase, I would say this preacher and his church suffered from low self-esteem. In their thinking, because they weren't big, they weren't successful or healthy or effective.

I saw a different picture. I saw a man who loved the people in his church and community. I saw a church and a community who loved the preacher. I saw good things happening in that ministry.

Still, it's hard to overcome the "smaller" stigma.

Transforming Our Communities

But wait a minute. Think about the vital role played by the thousands of smaller churches in smaller communities across North America. In every community people need to know Jesus Christ. In every community people need to be discipled. They need the fellowship of the saints. They need to be nurtured and loved and encouraged in their Christian faith. From weddings to funerals, from family problems to social concerns, from national crises to personal victories, people in every community need the ministry of the local church, no matter how small that community—or church—may be.

These needs speak to the importance of smaller churches in small communities across the land. Still, many leaders and volunteers in smaller churches feel unimportant and ineffective.

Do you feel like that?

It doesn't have to be that way. We can change the way we feel about our ministries—and the way we go about them.

Richard Baxter remained in the village of Kidderminster for fourteen years. I can only imagine what he must have thought when he entered that community and saw how ungodly and profane its people were. Did he think about packing up and leaving? Did he despair over the difficult task ahead of him? Did he think he wasn't the man to do the job? I don't know what he thought, but I know he stayed. And that profane community was totally changed as a result.

It happened then and it can happen today.

Let me ask you this: what do you think would happen if leaders and volunteers in smaller churches all across North America agreed on a simple plan—to transform their communities for Jesus Christ? What if the folks in your church agreed to stick together, to love each other like family, and to do whatever it takes to carry out that simple plan?

Can you imagine the collective difference this would make across our country? Can you imagine how many lives would be transformed? How many families kept together? Can you imagine how many schools and school boards, how many town and city councils—and subsequently community decisions—could be impacted across the nation by Christians and churches that chose to be salt and light to their communities?

Effective Churches Come in All Sizes

It's time for more basketball trivia. Earl Boykins has been called one of the Denver Nuggets' best clutch performers. In a January 2005 game against the division-leading Seattle Supersonics, Boykins nailed only one of six shots, a three-pointer, during his twenty-two minutes of game time. But in overtime play Boykins hit four out of five shots from the field (including one three-pointer) and six out of seven from the free-throw line. His tally of fifteen points in an overtime period broke the previous fourteen-point NBA record held for twenty-one years by Indiana's Butch Carter.

Boykins's performance was impressive by any standard—perhaps more so because at a mere five feet five inches tall, he set this record as the shortest player in the NBA.

Earl Boykins had no control over his height—that's a matter of genetics. But he didn't let that keep him from his pursuit of excellence. He accepted his genetic limitations, put forth his best effort, and became an NBA star.

This principle applies to churches and ministries too. If you're serving a smaller church, perhaps in a smaller community, don't let that stop you from seeing the big picture—the value of your ministry and the collective worth of your work for the kingdom of God. Just as some people are born with certain genetic limitations, your church may be facing certain limitations too—like geographical location and population. You may not have the influx of new families into your community or a steady stream of visitors in your worship service like churches located in rapidly growing regions of the country. But you can still excel in ministry given those limitations. You can be a healthy, vibrant, and effective congregation regardless of the size of your membership.

That's what this book is all about.

Many Writers, Many Experiences

This book was written to help unleash the potential that exists in smaller churches everywhere—to show that smaller churches all across the country are doing significant things for the kingdom of God and transforming their communities as a result. It was written to show that you and your church can have a similar impact on your community.

Fourteen writers from thirteen states have contributed to this project. Most are serving in smaller churches. Each writes from a unique perspective about a unique area of ministry.

If you're part of a smaller church, you will identify with the struggles and limitations these writers and their churches have faced. And you'll rejoice in their successes as they have overcome obstacles common to smaller churches and are making an eternal impact on their communities.

I've made some exceptions too. A few of the churches whose ministries are featured in this book have average worship attendances above two hundred. I've included them because they have unique stories to tell, and because they once belonged in the smaller churches category. In fact, one of the main reasons these churches have grown significantly is because they faithfully carried out their vision for their community while they were still smaller congregations.

Let's Get Personal—and Practical!

I hope you find this book intensely practical. I hope it gives you the motivation and tools you need to help your church make a lasting and eternal impact on your community.

The chapters in this book are at the same time self-contained and interrelated. Individually they offer living, breathing, contemporary examples of how a smaller church has taken on a specific ministry and excelled in that area. In that sense, each chapter stands alone as a valuable ministry resource. Together they paint a challenging portrait of what the church—any church— your church—can be in its community.

To help you identify with the churches and ministries featured in this book, each chapter comes with a brief profile of the congregation and community from which the author writes. Each of the churches represented in these chapters has a story to tell. You'll discover how each congregation recognized the need to develop its unique ministry, and you'll discover the conditions, observations, and biblical insights that led to the recognition of the need. (You might even be pleased to learn that several of the ministries featured in this book did not come about through years of careful planning, but were actually responses to felt needs.) You'll learn how these congregations developed the goals and strategies to meet the needs they identified. You'll gain insight into the process each congregation employed to achieve its goals and fulfill its strategy. You'll identify with the struggles they faced and the resistance they encountered. You'll be inspired by their endurance and perseverance. You'll see the results of their efforts and hear about their plans for the future.

But that's not all. Because this book was written to lead you and your church to action, each chapter calls for a response from the reader. Each writer concludes with an advice segment containing the author's response to the question, "Based on your experience, what advice would you give to leaders and volunteers in smaller churches across the country who would like to do something similar to what you have done?" The action segment which follows answers the question, "Where do I go from here?" It contains a series of practical steps you and your church can take to implement the ministries featured in each chapter.

Interested? It's time to see what we can learn.

END NOTES

[1] The Barna Update: "Small Churches Struggle to Grow Because of the People They Attract" (The Barna Group, Ltd., September 3, 2003), www.barna.org.

[2] Ibid.

[3] David Smithers, "Prayer Makes History," www.watchword.org/smithers/ww49a.htm.

[4] Leonard Ravenhill, "Richard Baxter of Kidderminster, DAYSPRING (Bethany House Publishers, 1963).

[5] Ibid.

CHAPTER TWO

PASSION, PRAYER, AND PLANNING—
CULTIVATING A CLIMATE FOR GROWTH

DAVID BYCROFT

WOW, WAS I EXCITED!

I had just returned from a church growth conference and was full of ideas and optimistic goals.

What I didn't understand was that the people in our church had not heard all the inspiring classes and were not ready to hear my lofty goals.

You should also understand the condition of the little burg where our church is located. Tyro, Kansas, is not unlike thousands of small towns across America. It had some glory days in the early 1900s during the oil boom, but as bigger and better oil fields were discovered to the south, Tyro began a slow, perpetual death. When I arrived in 1969, Tyro had a population of two hundred fifty and boasted a grocery store and a gas station. Within a few years, both had disappeared. With no McDonald's and no Wal-Mart, it was far from a place where anyone would imagine catching a vision of growing a church.

So when I boldly announced on the Sunday following the church conference that one day this church of less than one hundred would be running five hundred in attendance, I wasn't surprised when someone laughed out loud.

I never knew who laughed, but that incident became a "God moment." I decided then and there—just you wait and see!

No one is laughing today.

Today the Tyro Christian Church averages more than nine hundred for worship each Sunday. Our aggressive leadership led us in building a new auditorium in the year 2000 that can accommodate more than three thousand in multiple services. Our elders consistently discuss what it will take in order to reach that number of souls for the Lord in this area.

This growth, from an average of forty in 1969 to nine hundred in 2005, has been slow but steady. Our average attendance has increased by nearly twenty-five people a year over the past thirty-five years.

The Beginning of a Vision

"Now to him who is able to do immeasurably more than all we ask or imagine, according to his power that is at work within us" (Ephesians 3:20).

Ever since my mountaintop experience at the church conference, Ephesians 3:20 has become my daily motivator. God began to open my eyes to the possibilities of growing a great church in a small town.

Even after the conference I could not envision a church of one thousand in little Tyro, Kansas.

I was convinced that we could run five hundred, yet my hardest task at that time was to change the minds of the leadership and congregation. In its best days, this church had about one hundred fifty in attendance. Thanks to former minister Kenny Boles (now a professor at Ozark Christian College), the seeds of growth had already been sown in the minds of two of the elders.

Although they were not leading the church with growth in mind, they understood that the mission of the church is to reach the lost. As a result, they became the leaders I would need to help move us forward with vision. These two men were responsible for leading the congregation from an average attendance of forty to five hundred. I cannot overestimate the value and help these two men provided, even with their conservative views of finances and change.

God began to open my eyes to the possibilities of growth. Most of our non-farm workers had jobs in surrounding towns. Coffeyville, Caney, and Independence are within a fifteen-mile radius of Tyro. These towns accounted for a major portion of our county's population of forty thousand.

As I began to preach the Great Commission, our members who worked in those towns started inviting the people they knew to come to church with them. Exciting things began to happen. We learned that excitement attracts people and causes them to want to invite others. People began coming from other towns in the area.

We began to see greater possibilities. Years ago we realized that if we reached only 1 percent of the forty thousand people in our county, we would have four hundred in attendance. Today our leaders think in terms of reaching 10 percent of our county's population.

In the early days of our growth, it was tough to get people to drive five miles to church. Today nearly one-third of our members drive twenty-five miles or more to attend. People in our region today think nothing of driving once a week to Tulsa, Oklahoma (about eighty miles), to eat or shop. To them, a twenty-five-mile drive to church seems perfectly acceptable. As a result, our population base continues to grow. The basic principle here is that people are willing to drive as far to church on Sunday as they do to work each day.

Reaching the Lost

As our church began to grow, we put more and more emphasis on reaching people who were outside of Christ.

I dedicated one evening a week, from 5 to 9 PM or later, to calling on people and presenting the gospel to them. Although some of my methods have changed, I still do this some thirty-five years later—although now I make phone calls first to make sure people will be home. I seldom—in fact almost never—run into people who are offended that I show up at their houses. If it's a bad time, I excuse myself and set a time to come back later.

I also arrange studies with people that last from three to five weeks, rather than making a one-time shot at trying to win them.

We scheduled calling nights for the congregation. It was a struggle from the beginning to get our members to go calling, and it has remained that way. We have accomplished much with a monthly calling night, but it has never completely lost its awkwardness.

I became convinced that the best calling program was for Christians to engage people in spiritual conversations in their daily lives. Today we do not have an all-church calling program. Instead we encourage our people to witness on a daily basis through the normal contact they have with people at work, school, or play.

One of the most freeing concepts for our members, which has helped them become involved in personal evangelism, was to take what they love to do and use it as a tool to reach their friends for Christ. If you enjoy golf, use those occasions to influence those you are playing with to consider Jesus. I enjoy antique tractor pulls. Through my involvement in this pastime, I have baptized four people and sown seeds with many others. These were people completely outside of my normal realm of influence—until I started using what I love to do as an opportunity to witness for Christ.

We plan special events our people can use as opportunities to invite people. We schedule these events at the church building and away from it. Some people may never come to a church building, but will go to an event at a neutral location.

On-Site Facts

Some of the programs at our building include:

- A resurrection pageant (We have had up to three thousand in attendance in four performances.)

- Special concerts
- VBS carnival (More lost people come to this than any other events.)
- Revival meetings

Revival meetings continue to be an integral part of who we are as a church and the basis of much of our growth. In the early years, our twice-a-year, week-long revivals were the main harvest tool for our church. It was not uncommon for us to have thirty or forty additions in one week. As we became more effective in reaching people throughout the years, these numbers began to diminish. Today, if we have five to ten additions during a revival week, we consider that good. Our revival meetings give our people opportunities to invite their lost friends. These meetings also provide a new list of prospects to begin working on for Christ.

Although by most people's standards we still have great attendance at our revivals, by our standards it has gone downhill. Once we would have doubled our Sunday morning attendance during a revival; today we average about 60 percent of our Sunday morning attendance.

We attribute this to the fact that people have become so busy with activities and responsibilities that at best we can expect most to come only two or three times during a six-night event. We also have shortened one of our two annual revivals to Sunday through Wednesday instead of all week.

Often during revivals we invite guest evangelists who are effectively reaching the lost where they serve. We use them to teach our people at breakfast and luncheon meetings about their views on church growth and witnessing. Our members find these meetings inspiring.

Another tool we use during our revival meetings is the leadership calling night held the week before the meetings begin. On Tuesday and Thursday of that week we serve an evening meal for the staff, elders, and deacons. My wife, Kathy, graciously prepares and serves this meal in our home. After the meal we form groups of two and go out to call on people who need to make decisions for Christ.

During a week of revival, it is often hard to find people at home and have time to visit them between their arrival home from work and the time the meeting begins. Calling on our prospects the week before makes catching these people at home much easier.

On Wednesday night, the week before revival, we ask each leader to recruit a calling partner from the congregation and call on members who are not attending. This way, all nonattending members are visited at least two times a year. Dessert is served when the callers finish their task (courtesy of my wife again). At the end of these three calling nights, we share reports about each visit.

Vacation Bible School also brings new people to our church every year. We continue to try new approaches and methods to see how we can get our people to reach out and bring area kids. It is our prayer that the kids, in turn, will bring their families. After VBS is over, every unchurched child receives a visit from his or her VBS teacher or one of the staff members.

Off-Site Events

Our off-site events are designed for making contact with the lost rather than for preaching and teaching. These fun, nonthreatening gatherings allow our people to invite and rub shoulders with unbelievers. This also helps unbelievers see that Christians are normal people too. The goal of these events is to help lost people become more comfortable with the idea of attending a church service.

Whole Hog Roast

A couple of men in our church use a giant cooker to prepare mouth-watering barbecue. A farmer in our church donates a couple of hogs each year for this event held at the Tyro city park. Our people provide the side dishes for this huge picnic. We invite a music group to entertain us with gospel music. We ask them not to preach—just sing and have fun. At the end of the evening, I thank everyone for coming and invite the visitors to our church services.

July Fourth Week Fireworks

Our church co-ops with the city of Tyro to buy a fireworks display to be shown on the Wednesday closest to July 4. We do not try to compete with the major fireworks displays in the surrounding towns that take place on the July 4. We plan a patriotic service with music and a speaker, emphasizing God and country. After the service we serve homemade ice cream and desserts. At dark, people make their way to our parking lots with lawn chairs and blankets to enjoy the fireworks.

Galilean Service

A nearby lake provides the setting for this beautiful evening. After a hamburger cookout and carry-in style dinner, we settle on the banks of the lake.

A boat with an eight-foot lighted cross moves slowly across the lake. As it comes toward the shore where we are sitting, the congregation sings songs about the cross. A group of singers on the boat begins to sing as the boat draws near. We preach about the cross at this event, and visitors have always been moved by this.

Trap Shoot

Each team must consist of one church member and one nonmember. Trophies are awarded. This is a fun event.

Golf Scramble

Our golfers enjoy this. A team of four must consist of two from the church and two nonmembers. We play at a local golf course and cater a meal. We ask our members to pay the fees for their guests. The church helps with half of the green fees and pays for guest meals. We bring in a known athlete to share his testimony at the close of this event.

Softball

A couple in our church donated land for a softball diamond. We have our own league. We allow area churches to play in our league as well. We try to mix up the teams, with half the players from the church and half from outside the church. Presently we have five teams from our church and four teams from area churches in our summer league.

Car Show

Several men in our congregation show their rebuilt, classic cars on a regular basis in other towns. I asked them if they would like to put on a car show in Tyro, using our church parking lot for the car display area.

These men went all out! We had seventy cars at our first show. The following year we had more than one hundred fifty. The majority of participants are nonchurched people. We make it a fun day with lots of food, a DJ playing '60s music, and regular giveaways.

At the end of the show, after all the judging has taken place, the people go into our auditorium for the awards ceremony. I emcee this part of the event, which gives me opportunity to connect with the group. Our car show has opened doors to share the gospel with many who are outside of Christ.

Sho-De-O

This is a light version of a rodeo. Cowboys and cowgirls from our church stage the event and participate in it. This attracts a lot of new people, although it is hard work.

Events are set up to allow different age groups to compete. Our advertising is directed to those to outside of the church. A free meal is served to participants and the audience.

When it comes to the events we use to reach the unchurched, we look at activities our people are already involved in and then encourage them to use their talents, along with what they love to do, to reach people for Christ.

Attitude Adjustments

I can still remember a harsh encounter I had with one of the elders after I had changed the order of service for the first time. In my inexperience I was completely caught off guard when he pointed at my chest and said, "Young man, don't come in here changing things around. We like things just as they are."

Probably this mindset is found in many older, established churches—especially those in small-town America. I only wish I had understood the problem sooner. It would have saved many sleepless nights!

What I dealt with then, and what many of you who are reading this book are facing today, is simply a lack of maturity. Selfishness permeates every area of our lives, and sadly, the church is not exempt. The old catch phrase "Have it your way" seems to apply to more than fast-food restaurants. In other words, change often comes slowly in the smaller church. Our job is to help people see that it's not about us; it's about God. It's not what makes me happy or comfortable, but what pleases him.

Disagreements over musical styles and preferences are among the most controversial issues churches face. Opinions fly freely. Sometimes tempers flare. Rarely do people stop and ask "What kind of music does God want?" Seldom are we urged to study Ephesians 5:19 or Psalm 150 to recognize how God would like to be worshiped. Mature Christians can be led through change without having to be dragged along kicking and screaming.

We had the luxury of starting a new time for worship when we needed to add a second service. This new service used a full band, drums and all. That meant no one had to adjust his or her preference of musical style. People could choose the early service or remain with the late service where the music style was unchanged. We then added a third service, sandwiched between our original service times, and used the new service to launch our praise band service. Immediately it became our most well-attended service, and it has continued to grow. About six months into this format, one of our more conservative elders addressed the issue at an elders' meeting. "I want everyone to know that I hate the music in the worship band service," he said. "However, I have never seen anything attract more young families than this has, and I think we need to keep doing it!" Now that is maturity—being able to see past what you like or want in order for someone else to have his needs met.

Almost every difficult issue could be resolved more easily if we first asked "What does God want?" and then "How can we reach others?" When we die to self, the church functions much more efficiently. We must begin teaching these attitudes and let God change hearts, rather than forcing the issue and creating hostility.

The second major area of attitude adjustment is reflected in the expression "We've never done it that way before." Many of our churches are stuck in the 1950s. The '40s, '50s, and '60s were good years for our churches. Look at how many church buildings were built during that time period. Unfortunately, many church leaders today equate those methods and programs exclusively with the blessings of God.

They have blended the methods with the message of God's Word and made the methods as sacred as the Word. When someone attempts change by elimination of the old ways or addition of some new methods, the troops often get restless.

Again, it is a matter of maturity—placing the will of God and his message above the will of men, their methods and traditions. This truth will have to be slowly and carefully taught to an established congregation in order to bring them to a willingness to let go of some of their sacred cows. When leaders try to force change too quickly, the result is anarchy. If, however, you use God's Word to instruct and challenge the congregation to mature thinking, you can slowly and steadily change a church.

Some of our 1950s methods simply will not work in our present culture. I mentioned revivals earlier. In the '40s and '50s, most families had five or six free nights a week. Since there were few outlets for finding outside entertainment, it wasn't hard to get people to come to a church building to hear an outstanding preacher, listen to a music group, or watch a chalk artist. Today, many families are engaged in outside activities nearly every evening. And they can choose from several forms of entertainment each night. It's tough to get a crowd out during the week. I'm not suggesting that we eliminate revivals; but we ought to rethink what we are trying to accomplish. Perhaps some different approaches are in order. Some churches today are investing their time and resources in events such as Easter pageants and Christmas services with outstanding results. It's time we rethought our delivery methods of the gospel.

I was holding a revival in Illinois where I met a church family who operated a business making, packaging, and selling steak sauce. The man who is the head of the company told me that they were in the process of changing their bottle from glass to plastic. In shipping costs alone they would save one hundred fifty thousand dollars a year. The contents in the bottle had not changed; only the container changed. What if someone in the company had said, "We've sold our sauce in glass bottles since this company began. It was good enough for my dad, it was good enough for me, so it's good enough for you"? That company would have lost one hundred fifty thousand dollars annually. They would have been less competitive in the market, resulting in even more loss.

Most of our churches need to look at their packaging of the gospel. Are there better delivery methods? Let's consider some new and inviting methods without compromising the contents of the gospel. Methods change, but the message doesn't.

What About Prayer?

E. M. Bounds wrote, "Nothing is done well without prayer for the simple fact that it leaves God out of the account and becomes a human effort alone."

Those words challenge me to seek God's help, direction, and power. Otherwise, I am merely building a sand castle that will wash away with the tide of the next generation.

Prayer starts with the preacher, spreads through the leadership, and is caught by the congregation. I have established an e-mail prayer group to whom I send prayer thoughts and requests every day. Most people will pray if they know what to pray about.

Instead of directing all our prayers toward the physically sick, how about praying for those who are spiritually sick? Challenge your people to pray for the lost, for new methods of reaching people, and for upcoming programs. If you put the needs in front of the people, they will pray. If you lead your people to become people of prayer, many of your new methods will be more easily introduced and accepted.

Prayer is our recognition that it is by God's power—not our own talents and hard work—that growth results.

Developing Leaders

I wish I had started sooner than I did to develop leaders. When young preachers complain to me about their immature leaders and what they do, they are seldom satisfied with my answer: leaders are not going to be developed overnight. Still, that is what most of us want. We want five easy steps to develop dynamic spiritual leaders in six months or less!

I can, however, promise substantial growth in one year.

Look for and pray for three to six men who are currently leading or have leadership potential. Ask them to meet with you once a week for a year. I have done this at various times—early in the morning before work, over the lunch hour, or in the evening. For me, it works out best to meet in the early morning.

Use published material in your study or develop your own—just make sure it will challenge the members of your group to grow spiritually. Weave concepts of biblical leadership throughout your discussions. Within a year, you will be able to see who is rising to the top and who is going through the motions. You may find that you have one or more men who will accept the challenge to lead their own group the following year. This will multiply your ability to raise up future leaders.

About four years ago I started a group called Master's Men. I sent out one hundred letters to new men in the church or men who had been in the church for years but were not involved. I prayed for fifty men to accept the challenge of meeting once a month for a year. Fifty-two accepted the challenge. They agreed not to miss a meeting unless it was an emergency. I finished the year with about thirty-five men who completed that challenge. We studied leadership material. At times I asked them to help with work projects. We drew names at the end of each meeting to pair up prayer partners for the coming month. The men shared requests with each other. I asked them to keep in contact with each other during the month. This allowed them to get to know one another on a more personal basis.

Since then I have worked with smaller groups and have found them more productive. The group I'm meeting with now has about fifteen men in it. These groups of men are the foundation of my e-mail prayer group. Several new deacons have been trained through this method, and I can see potential in several others who continue to build on that year of study.

The greatest development tool I have used with our present leaders is something I call the spiritual board meeting. In my early years with the church, our board meetings were little more than business meetings that opened and closed with prayer. So I challenged our leaders to meet one night a month exclusively for spiritual development.

We have used materials from many sources. Ben Merold has produced a series of videos on church growth I highly recommend. We have also used material from John Maxwell, Rick Warren, and Bob Russell. All of our discussions focus on ways to lead the Lord's church to do "immeasurably more than all we ask or imagine, according to his power that is at work within us" (Ephesians 3:20).

Without doubt, our spiritual board meetings have been the best thing we have done to keep our men growing and developing as dynamic spiritual leaders. Today, every elder we have has been through all these materials I have mentioned. That's why they have a vision of reaching four thousand people in, of all places, Tyro, Kansas!

Consider Those Action Steps

1. Develop a prayer team that prays about:
   - leadership development.
   - reaching the lost (give them a specific goal).
   - the preacher and his sermons.

- the congregation to become mature enough to give up their rights so the lost can be reached.

2. Plan a leadership retreat and use some of the material I mentioned earlier. I strongly suggest using Ben Merold's videos.

3. Begin a monthly training meeting for your present leadership group.

4. Select a group and start developing future leaders (such as the Master's Men class).

5. Encourage present and future leaders to attend a church growth seminar.

6. Find a church that is twice your present size, or at least in the four hundred to five hundred range. Take your leaders there. Let their leadership challenge your men with what they are doing.

7. Establish a calling night for the sole purpose of reaching the lost and visiting newcomers. Never go alone—always take someone with you so you can do on-the-job training.

CHAPTER THREE

OUTREACH—
LOVING YOUR COMMUNITY

CURTIS SHELBURNE

STILL HAVE THE NOTE I RECEIVED SOME YEARS AGO FROM CHRISTIAN AUTHOR MAX LUCADO. I'd written to tell him how much his writing had meant to me and to comment on a bumpy spot in our friendship. (He wasn't aware we had a friendship, but I count myself among his several hundred thousand closest reader-friends!)

As I told Max, I had just boarded a Southwest Airlines jet. I opened his book, *A Gentle Thunder* (Word Publishing, 1995), before the plane left the gate. And then, right there on page three, Max had written, "A good pilot does what it takes to get his passengers home." How timely!

I flew through the pages, and the trip was going just fine until a crash of sorts—which had nothing to do with the airplane and everything to do with the book—jarred me in chapter four. Max was illustrating the fact that not all of life is glitzy and glamorous.

The honeymoon ends.

The IRS calls.

Or the boss calls and wants you to spend a week in Muleshoe, Texas.

That hurt! You see, I was a resident—by choice—of Muleshoe, Texas, and had served a church there for more than a decade. I admitted to Max that you can't live in a town called Muleshoe and be too squeamish about jokes relating to the town's unusual name. When (unlike Max) I receive book manuscript rejections, I can imagine publishers wondering, *Can any good thing come out of Muleshoe?*

Well, it can.

As I told Max, I wasn't all that ticked about his slight to our fair city; I just thought the symmetry of his writing and my reading that day was remarkable! I closed my note with a warm expression of thanks (and forgiveness), and he must have liked it because he replied, "Your note made my day!"

Muleshoe really is a well-kept secret. Our town (population four thousand five hundred) is a great place to raise a family. My wife and I have raised four sons here. It's a great place to serve a church and even to try to write an occasional paragraph or two.

Did I mention that Muleshoe is a lot like Malibu? Both start with an *M* and end with an *ooh*, and aside from a conspicuous absence in Muleshoe of breathtaking ocean cliff views and sea breezes, the two towns are quite similar

Have a hard time believing that? OK. But my family and I do thank God for the twenty years he's given us here. No matter what our society says, bigger is not necessarily better.

Like the town we live in, the church we serve is not large. Established in 1969, our congregation has never been large (one hundred twenty-five or so showed up on Sunday mornings at its peak in the 1970s.) As our county's population has declined, so has our membership. We now have one hundred members on the books, but, of course, they never appear at the same time!

All of us know how hard it is to grow a church when population trends are challenging. Demographics affect every group in any area, whether we're talking about churches or fast-food restaurants. While we can't do much about our community's demographics, we can do a lot about being a spiritually healthy church. In expanding or declining communities, great churches come in all sizes. (So do sick ones.) A healthy smaller church has a huge potential for genuine growth in ways that truly matter.

This region of Texas is heavily agricultural, and we have rarely experienced a more prosperous time than during our congregation's formative years. We began small, but that economic boom led to generosity that resulted in a fine physical church plant and parsonage—bought, built, and paid for long before I came on the scene.

Our smaller church status can partially be explained by the fact that our congregation traces its roots to a splinter group in our larger tradition. Congregations in this small group have tended to be smaller and less affluent than those in the mainstream of our brand. Ancient issues that separated us have faded (thank God), and I have experienced in this smaller congregation a freedom in Christ that many of my colleagues in larger, more traditional churches find amazing. But we still face some unique challenges because of our stunted historical roots.

One challenge is obvious. Our church is small. People who have eyes only for large are largely blind to the blessings the Lord can offer through a smaller church. They seldom take time to find out what a great church we are. So we remain a smaller church, but a great church.

Our church is not the "First Church" of its brand in our community. Even without a sign that says so, everyone in town knows which congregation that is. And we aren't it—which means you probably wouldn't visit our church first if you moved to town.

Did I mention that, not being the biggest church in our small community, we don't have anything that could be mistaken for a big youth group, a big budget, or a big staff?

Did I mention that when I moved here, I knew this church had about as much chance of morphing into a megachurch as Saddam Hussein has of becoming an ordained Southern Baptist missionary?

And yet . . .

And yet if you were to visit Muleshoe and ask people about our unimposing church, you'd find we may have the best reputation in town as a church that deeply loves its community. If a little church like ours—one that started with two strikes against it—can be esteemed so highly by its neighbors, surely yours can too!

What are some of the factors the Lord has used to lead our church to this positive position? And what might he call you to do in your own community as you look for effective ways to share the love of Christ?

Good questions. But first let me share one word of caution. Every church is unique. What works in Muleshoe, Texas, might not fly in Donkeyhoof, Montana. So be wise in implementing any suggestions I offer.

How does a church go about truly loving its community?

First of all, I believe that *loving your community means inviting them in.* Making yourself vulnerable by choosing to deal with real needs and really coming to love those you're working with can cost time and dollars and tears. The most important—and costly—investment in our communities is the one we make when we invite people into our hearts.

But even inviting the community into your building can be a bit messy. About thirty years ago our church added on a nicer-than-usual fellowship hall. Soon after it was built, a lively discussion took place about restrictions on its use. One leader made a statement that speaks volumes about whether a church truly loves its community. "We want to take care of this place," he acknowledged, "but must not make restrictions that keep the community out. We want them to come in!"

Here are a few ideas about ways to invite your neighbors in.

Fellowship, Food, and Informational Programs

Who doesn't love to eat? Our church is great at fulfilling that need. We have some unbelievably fine cooks. We used their talents to provide a highly successful program we called Soup and Sandwich. People in our community love to get together. So once a month, on third Thursdays, we invited anyone in town to join us for a freewill offering meal and an enjoyable program. We sent out a list of the programs for the year, put a note in the newspaper each month, asked businesses to post reminders, and invited everybody to come. Our menu was soup and sandwiches only once; after that the meals just got bigger and better. In August we had the school superintendent talk about the coming year. A local minister usually spoke before Easter. The high school choir sang carols in December. Once or twice a year local singing groups and musicians serenaded us (always our most popular programs). Our "clientele" included all sorts, but particularly retired folks and business people who wanted a good lunch and program packed into the lunch hour. A small town is perfect for this sort of thing. The people in our community loved it.

Benevolence Programs

One day the school nurse called one of our elders, who is also our school superintendent. She was concerned about low-income kids who couldn't afford winter coats. He consulted with a lady in our congregation who is also our city's economic development director, and together they launched our church's annual holiday coat drive. Every fall we use our local newspaper, TV station, and flyers to invite townspeople to donate coats that are collected in boxes at several businesses. Then in November we have a coat distribution day at our church and invite anyone who needs a winter coat to come get one. We may be a smaller church, but in two years we've given away more than one thousand coats!

Special Needs Programs

Over the years we've made available to the community video studies on child-rearing, discipline, and adolescence (from Focus on the Family and other organizations). We're presently asking for volunteers to lead a divorce-recovery group. We hosted an estate-planning seminar taught by an attorney, the daughter of one of our members. Soon we will offer programs on debt reduction and financial planning. We are dreaming of a program that would provide after-school reading assistance for latchkey and other kids.

Loving your community means finding creative and beneficial ways to invite them in!

Loving your community also means getting out among the people.

Opportunities for service outside our doors also are numerous and varied. I'll mention a few—and I hereby tip my hat to some colleagues who told me what their churches are doing in this regard.

Welcome and Thank You Programs

We use a pie ministry to welcome folks who are new to our town and visit our church. One of our ladies bakes a pie. Then either she or another volunteer takes the pie and some information about our church and makes a brief visit that says "We're glad you're here!" One friend told me about his church's cookie ministry. Every month this ministry committee bakes cookies for a different group: doctors, nurses, hospital staff, nursing home staff and residents, teachers, pharmacists, police, volunteer firemen, EMTs. Simple, yes, but greatly appreciated.

Aid and Support to Community Programs

Another colleague confirmed my own experience. He said it makes more sense for a smaller church to support existing food, housing, and medical programs than to create new programs of their own. While serving in existing programs, our members wind up working alongside folks from other churches, thereby learning to love them more as together they glorify Christ. Members of your congregation could assist in Meals on Wheels, Habitat for Humanity, food banks, hospice, prescription or utility aid programs, homeless or battered women shelters, foster children advocacy programs, and so on. Involving your members in these ministries sends a community-wide signal that your church believes in reaching out in practical Christian love.

Other Cooperative Community Church Programs

Most communities have a ministerial association. Sometimes these organizations can become political or controversial, but the ones I've worked with have been encouraging and productive. They may provide valuable services such as transient aid, and most ministers find making contacts with other ministers to be a blessing to themselves, their churches, and their communities.

Many ministerial associations sponsor community worship services. Our church plays a key role in these services, and this has been a key factor in the positive reputation we enjoy in our town.

Words of Advice

Perhaps some variation of these programs could work for you, but no one knows better than you what will bless your church and your community.

With your indulgence, though, may I offer some advice that may be even more helpful? It might be fun to present this in a David Letterman Top Ten format, although the only item in the order of priority is the last one, which truly is No. 1. If you prefer, dump Letterman and opt for Moses as we call the following ideas Ten Commandments for Loving Your Community.

Number 10: One size never fits all.

I'm a Big & Tall kind of guy, so I can say with deep feeling (and a hint of animosity toward manufacturers who perpetrate the one-size-fits-all myth) that what is true of airplane seats and sock sizes is far truer of churches and church programs: one size *never* fits all.

Lyle E. Schaller in *The Small Church Is Different!* (Abingdon, 1982) makes a great case that smaller churches are as different from larger churches as rutabagas are from bananas, or as pumpkins are from horses! As Schaller writes, "The person who is very competent in raising pumpkins may not be an expert in caring for horses." And different criteria are used for judging a pumpkin than for appraising a horse. Smaller churches are *not* miniature replicas of large churches. They are different organisms! We who lead in ministry must not let our need to be seen as "successful" ministers cause us to put our poor congregations through hoops they were never meant to jump. It's God's kingdom we want to grow—not ours.

Number 9: Celebrate what's already happening before adding new programs.

Sometimes we're too close to the trees to see the forest. Your church may already be loving your community in some marvelous ways. Before adding programs, take inventory of what your church is already doing well. One of my most committed members serves as the activity director at our local nursing home. She is gratefully recognized by our entire community as a person truly gifted by God. We'd be insane to plan a church program to duplicate what she is already doing.

Number 8: Don't overprogram your people.

All churches, especially smaller ones, need to be careful about multiplying programs. We tend to ride our best volunteers into the ground.

One wise minister tells me that in his congregation "our best community ministry has been the involvement of individual members in key community efforts," rather than in specific congregational ministries. This small-but-good church wants their people to have time to serve on the board of United Way, the school board, the local food bank, YMCA youth sports, Rotary and other service clubs, the local Christian counseling center, Gideons, scouting, Mended Hearts, and similar organizations. So their church intentionally limi order to make outside commitments possible. As this colleag be 'the salt of the earth' if you're confined to the saltshaker."

Let's be honest! Your smaller church will never win a p larger church; and if you try, you'll drive yourself, your fellow ... longsuffering members crazy—and away. You cannot offer a support group for left-handed thirty-two-year-old redheaded secretaries born in months ending in *R*s! So what? I doubt your appliance store on Main Street can compete with Wal-Mart's prices. But they can offer service Wal-Mart can't touch. And your smaller church may offer a quality of relationships and genuine support some larger churches can only dream of!

Number 7: Focus on quality rather than quantity.

Leaders of smaller churches are wise to know enough about their particular strengths and the gifts of their members to choose a few programs they can do well for the long haul. So what if a church growth guru bragged about a Honolulu church that used underwater basket-weaving as an outreach tool to Maui pearl divers? Keep things simple and do what your church can do well.

Number 6: Don't be greedy for numerical growth.

All growth is not numerical, and spiritual growth matters most. But, alas, the only kind of growth some people care about is numerical.

I want my church to grow in every way, but I am convinced that size has little to do with whether a church is a great church. Your job in your corner of the kingdom is to be faithful—whether your congregation grows numerically or not. If you are faithful to the Lord, then everything you do honors Christ, blesses his kingdom, and in some way enlarges its boundaries.

Blessed is the church and her leaders who do all they do to build God's kingdom and do not worry about building their own! How blessed are those who know the difference between God's kingdom and their own!

Number 5: Realize that lasting growth is often slow growth.

For more than thirty-five years, our little church has been loving its community. Consequently we are known and loved by our community. Numerically our membership has not changed much. The Lord has surprised us at times with wonderful additions. But the solid growth we've seen over the years has come because of the longstanding relationships that flourish in smaller communities. Several of our members came into our church because we were there for them in a crisis time. Others belonged to neighboring ches that sadly went through turmoil, and these people suddenly needed safe place to worship the Lord. We try hard not to steal sheep, but these good folks needed a refuge. They knew that although we have retained the brand name on our church sign, we try to be a community church. Some came because they needed a deeper relationship with the Lord, and they knew we weren't just counting scalps. But growth like this can't happen overnight any more than a mature oak tree can spring up in the morning sun.

Number 4: Keep the home fires burning as you reach outside.

Is outreach important? Of course. But to have something worth giving when you reach out, you must keep your own spiritual batteries charged. Isn't this what Jesus did when he went out to a quiet place by himself and prayed?

Churches need both discipleship and outreach. In our pragmatic, program-oriented, and results-obsessed society, worship time may be disdained because it is not overtly productive in building numbers, but William Willimon and Robert Wilson are right when they say that "pastors of small-membership churches . . . need to view preaching and worship leadership as their primary pastoral activities." Other activities and outreach are important, but these church experts insist that "small churches need to see the Sunday service of their church as their primary activity."

Number 3: Recognize the crucial role of your minister as a leader and model in loving your community.

I believe a small-church minister's primary roles are preaching and leading worship, but a significant part of his work is also to represent the church to the community. It is crucial to your church's success that he be supported, empowered, and encouraged in this role.

Ask yourself: am I pleased to introduce this person to my neighbors as my minister? Am I glad he's "ours" and that everyone in town knows it? Your love and encouragement are basic to your minister's success and longevity. Do I need to tell you that a church that goes through seven preachers in ten years will have little influence in its community?

If you have a successful minister, encourage him. Support him emotionally and financially so that he wants to stay and can afford to stay. Do you really want the cheapest preacher you can get? Can your church afford that?

Number 2: Realize what separatism says to your community.

Christians rub shoulders with community folks at the grocery store, the bank, football games, and the local coffee shop. You don't have to agree on every issue to enjoy and bless one another. I wonder why some Christians believe they should not also worship alongside these same people? Those who take this stance need to realize what they are saying—whether they mean to or not—to their community. Separatism is as deadly to community love as grease is to soap bubbles!

The leaders in my congregation not only want me to interact with other ministers and churches in town, they want me to help plan and lead community worship experiences. We have occasionally swapped pulpits with a large church from a different tradition. These pulpit swaps may be the most eloquent sermon we preach to those who have been turned off to Jesus by the fussing of his followers.

Now, may I ask for a drum roll, please? (Or, if you opted for Moses over Letterman, perhaps a trumpet blast or two.) Here is Commandment Number One for the church that truly desires to love its community:

Number 1: Understand that you must be able to say "we" and mean it.

In one of his "News from Lake Wobegon" pieces, Garrison Keillor tells about Harold Starr, editor of tiny Lake Wobegon, Minnesota's *Herald-Star*. Harold is a great guy and a capable newspaper editor. People like Harold, and he's been in Lake Wobegon a good while now, which is important to the townspeople. The function and role of the *Herald-Star* is quite different from that of the *New York Times*. Occasionally Harold has to remind himself of this.

You see, Harold's subscribers in Lake Wobegon are far more interested in a picture of Mrs. Conway's fourth-grade class at the county spelling bee than they are in investigative reporting. If Harold had won a Pulitzer Prize because he had been the first to reveal the identity of Watergate's Deep Throat, most of his subscribers would say "Well, that's nice," skim the article, but really read the one about how the Diener boy placed second down at the state track meet or whose hog won Grand Champion over at the St. Cloud Stock Show. And Harold's readers really love those little four-liners such as, "Arlene Tornquist's daughter Anna-Louise visited this week from Minneapolis along with her dog Clarence." What matters most to his readers is that Harold can say "we" to them and mean it.

If your community realizes that you are glad to be an important part of them—that you stand with them and not self-righteously over them, that if they're cut you bleed, that if they rejoice you rejoice—then you have a God-given opportunity to spread Christ's love and seasoning influence throughout the community you love—and you'll find that they will love you back!

My family and I have been serving in Muleshoe, Texas for more than twenty years. I hoped when we came here that we'd be able to stay for a good while, but I never dreamed we would stay this long. Will we ever move away? I have no idea what the future holds. But I can testify that what God has done for our family in the past two decades has been more wonderful than anything I could have engineered or predicted. And I do know this: wherever we serve in the future, twenty years in this small town has been one of God's finest blessings to me and mine. From firsthand experience, I can say that ministering to a smaller church in a small community can be a very large blessing indeed.

CHAPTER FOUR

EVANGELISM—
FINDING A NICHE FOR SPREADING THE GOSPEL

MILTON JONES

NUMBERS. GOD MUST LOVE THEM OR ELSE WE WOULDN'T HAVE A BOOK IN OUR BIBLE BY THAT NAME. At times I really love numbers in evangelism. That's usually when the church is growing. At other times I don't want to hear about them. How much attention should we pay to numbers? God mentioned the three thousand in Acts 2. He also mentioned the shepherd leaving the numbers to look for one lost sheep. I try to be careful with numbers. There have been times when I declare their unimportance simply because I don't want to see reality so clearly. And yet at other times I tend to mention them more because of my pride than my passion for the lost.

How important are numbers for the smaller church? Too often churches with a smaller attendance are considered unsuccessful. However, numbers don't tell you that much about the health of a congregation unless they are applied to evangelism. Many smaller churches have been very effective in evangelism. On the other hand, some larger congregations have grown more by transfer and location than outreach. Evangelism can happen in a church of any size.

How much attention should smaller churches pay to the trends that seem to have an impact on the growth of the church? There are places, people groups, and periods of time that affect a church. Being on the cutting edge of certain trends can certainly help or hurt the size of a congregation. So when it comes to trends, how important are the numbers? I certainly think that we should be wise in the way we do our outreach. Devoting myself to a method that doesn't work can hardly be justified. But writing someone off just because he is in the minority hardly seems loving. On the other hand, if certain groups of people are open to the gospel, shouldn't we be there for them more than ever?

An Amazing Statistic

Having stated all that, let me tell you about the most amazing statistic on evangelism I have heard in years. When I first heard it, I didn't believe it. In fact, my skepticism was so great that I had to prove it to myself in order to believe it. It was just a few years ago when Paul Tans wrote his study called *Signs of the Times* that I became aware of this overwhelming statistic.

The statistic states that 95 percent of the people in America who become Christians do so before the age of twenty-five. Think about that. If we don't reach people with the gospel before they reach the age of twenty-five, we are going to miss 95 percent of them.

Why aren't we very evangelistic anymore? That is what so many people are asking. Why aren't churches growing more? Maybe the answer is simple—we aren't reaching young people.

As a result, the Northwest Church of Christ in Seattle decided to reach young people. The problem with a smaller church is that you can't do everything like a larger church. But you can do a few things—or maybe even just one thing—well. Northwest decided to get younger, more evangelistic, and develop a niche ministry. They were going to put their time, effort, and money into one ministry for the sake of evangelism—campus ministry.

The Northwest Church of Christ at the time had around seventy-five members and was nearly seventy-five years old. They were located in the heart of Seattle near Greenlake, about ten minutes from the University of Washington. It was a church with a rich history and had planted many churches in the past, but it had simply grown older over the last couple of decades. Most of the members were around sixty years old. There wasn't much of a youth group. In fact there weren't many children at all. It was full of a bunch of loving people who had simply arrived at a time when the glory days seemed to be a thing of the past.

Reaching a Younger Generation

Instead of giving up or closing the doors, the elders decided to recruit some young people to move to Seattle and start a campus ministry at the University of Washington. At the time, I was ministering in Lubbock, Texas, as a campus minister at Texas Tech University. Upon the church's invitation, I led seventeen young people from the Texas Tech ministry to Seattle to begin a new church-based campus ministry. I can't think of anything to invigorate a dying congregation more than an influx of young people and an intensive commitment to evangelism.

The exodus of students provided a rather unique fellowship. There were a lot of older people and a lot of college students, but there were hardly any middle-aged people or children in the church. Could this really work? Everyone knows that older people like the status quo and younger people want to rock the boat. Isn't that true? But these two groups committed to love each other, to be patient with one another, and to be flexible with their methodology.

The Northwest congregation knew it would have to change to reach out to younger people. Musical styles, programs, and traditions of decades past were going to have to be undone and renewed to connect with a new generation. It meant that the church wouldn't revolve around the old guard as much anymore. As surprising as it may seem, this older church opened the doors and let it happen. College students started coming to the church in droves. During the first two years, more than one hundred fifty students were baptized. Within only two years, there were more new students who were members of the congregation than there were older members.

When I look at outreach methods, events, and programs in the smaller church, most seem to be designed for people older than twenty-five. If that is true, we are going after only 5 percent of the open people when it comes to evangelism. I certainly want older people to be saved (I like people my age), but the truth is that most people my age and older have already made decisions one way or another. Should we still try and reach them? Absolutely. But what are we doing about the young?

Ask someone young at church to tell you what he or she thinks. I'm afraid many of our styles—from preaching to music to programs—may eclipse the gospel from young people. To be evangelistic today, we have to communicate the gospel in ways that young people actually hear. Young people need a voice in how we minister and worship if we are going to be serious about reaching their peers. And those of us who are older will have to decide whether we will allow change for the sake of the mission.

These statistics will prompt us to reconsider the importance of children's ministry, youth ministry, and campus ministry. And they also call us to examine whether these ministries in our churches are simply for us or primarily for the outsider. If our ministries to young people aren't outreach oriented, when will evangelism happen? Many of our churches could be getting smaller simply because we are waiting too late to reach young people.

Paul teaches us to preach the word "in season and out of season" (2 Timothy 4:2). In America the season seems to be related to a person's age. I want everyone to hear, but I especially want to get the word out when it is "in season."

Rethinking Our Methodology

After many years of success in reaching college students, a couple of years ago the Northwest congregation found itself once again not reaching many young people. In some ways we were like the church at Sardis. We had the reputation for reaching young people and thought we were doing a good job, but in actuality it wasn't happening anymore. So once again, we decided to put our money, efforts, and priorities into reaching the college students who had caused a renewal in our congregation in the past. This time, however, we found that the methods that had worked two decades ago in bringing revival weren't that effective in this present age.

We found that young people were not as interested in traditional campus ministries as they were open to being a part of what has been labeled "the emerging church." Our church had grown and was no longer a smaller church, but this bigger church was no longer reaching college students. As a result, we decided to plant a new church—a church within a church at our present location. In other words, we believed that we were going to have to become a smaller church in order to reach the young. So a few years ago, we started a new "church within a church" called Northwest Passage which meets on Sunday evenings. Its music, preaching, atmosphere, and order were drastically different from our other worship assemblies. However, we found that we could share ministries, groups, and leaders with our other assemblies. Even though it was designed for young people, we did not want this new church to be strictly a youth church. As a result, our elders and many older members committed to attending and fellowshiping with this new church. Many young people today are experiencing angst because of a failed relationship with a parent or a lack of a relationship with someone older. Many church plants today simply become generational churches of exclusively younger people. On the other hand, many established churches have evolved into older generational churches. We felt that if intergenerational healing is going to take place in our society, it should happen first in the church. Therefore, instead of asking the young to join the old, we asked the old to join the young for the purpose of support, mentoring, and wisdom.

Once again, Northwest Passage started reaching younger people, primarily college students who did not know Jesus Christ. Once again, we found that the church functioned best in evangelism when it was smaller.

We don't always keep people at our congregation for the long haul of their spiritual journey. Some of them transfer to larger churches because of unique ministries that exist only at larger congregations. Others move; college students often leave after four years to go to another place to find a job. However, these people tend to look back on our church as the church that led them to the Lord, the church that gave them their start on their walk with God. Evangelism and starting people off on their way is our niche in the kingdom in the Seattle area. And it has happened best as a smaller church. A part of me wishes all these people had stayed at Northwest. Then we would be a megachurch too. But maybe our place in the kingdom is to be the first door. When I realize that, it also helps me see larger churches not as competitors, but as a part of the kingdom, helping us mentor people on the far journey.

A Place to Grow Leaders

One of the unique aspects of the smaller church is leadership development. It is surprising how many leaders of larger churches developed leadership skills in a smaller church. When my son went off to college, he started attending a larger church. He wanted to play in a worship band and learn to be a better worship leader. After months of an interview process, he still hadn't made it into one of the worship bands. He went to another church that had a few hundred instead of several thousand and was leading worship his second week there. It wasn't that the larger church was bad; they simply had a large musical staff they needed to use. And it is hard for a larger church to take a chance on an unknown talent or provide a place where a young person can grow through his mistakes. A smaller church can provide that greenhouse where a younger person can grow to be a leader. Expectations of perfectly planned and executed assemblies are not a part of the typical smaller church. Where is a younger, inexperienced preacher going to hone his skills? It will not be in a large church. A smaller church can easily handle a mistake or someone who hasn't developed his talents yet. Therefore, smaller churches are needed for leadership development—not only to reproduce other smaller churches but also to supply leaders for larger churches. As a result, the smaller church can be very attractive to young people if it is willing to let that the younger person be involved in significant ministries.

Niche ministries come in a variety of shapes and sizes. Campus ministry was the niche ministry of the Northwest Church. But there are others that could work well for a smaller church. A Christian twelve-step program similar to Celebrate Recovery could reach out to a brand-new group. It would take a lot of help from many in the church to make it successful, but if it were prioritized, outsiders would be open to coming to such a niche ministry. Ministries like Divorce Care or a specialized youth or children's ministry would also work well.

Finding and Pursuing Your Niche

To get a niche ministry going, a church needs to pray about the diverse options or simply observe the various opportunities already existing. If a church were located near a campus, a college ministry would be a good idea. If the church is noticing a lot of people with addictions needing help, a recovery ministry might be the niche. For a successful start, the ministry needs to be identified by the whole church as a ministry that deserves attention, staffing, and support. The congregation needs to know that it will be a prioritized ministry for the sake of outreach. Everyone needs to understand how the entire congregation in one way or another is needed to support this ministry. To be successful, it will need to be a focus of the church for the long haul. The church will be identified by it. For instance, for decades the Northwest Church has been called by other people "the church with the campus ministry."

If a smaller church wanted to start a campus ministry like we did, it would require a commitment to change, a desire to grow younger, and a priority for evangelism. The church would have to invite some young people and experts in this ministry to join them. This would require some additional funding. It would be difficult to do a campus ministry without a campus minister. Impact Ministries is an international ministry of Christian Churches dedicated to planting campus ministries and encouraging young people to move to new campuses for evangelistic reasons. It would be a good contact for churches wanting to pursue this particular niche ministry. Many smaller churches are reluctant to hire more staff, but most niche ministries will require specific staffing, like a campus minister, and would necessitate the church to launch out with new faith in funding this ministry.

Smaller churches can also concentrate on niche mission efforts. Where the larger church may have many and diverse mission sites, a smaller church can focus on one area that becomes its specific mission. Recently, we dedicated ourselves to a certain area of Kenya. In a large church, if the focus on this specific region were mentioned so frequently, it would seem out of place or exclusive. However in our congregation, people love it because it has become the place where we send our members as short-term and long-term missionaries. We pray regularly and communicate extensively about this area of the world. Teens are encouraged to do summer mission work there. It has become our niche in the world for missions.

We did the same thing in benevolence. Northwest concentrated heavily on supporting AIDS orphans in sub-Sahara Africa through the Christian Relief Fund. Presently we support many more orphans than we have members. It is what we do when it comes to benevolence. No one gets tired of it. It is everyone's favorite ministry and is prioritized in all our communications and funding. Many other larger churches also help Christian Relief Fund, but no congregation owns the work more than we do; and we are able to do that because we are smaller and have chosen this to be a niche ministry of our church.

Every church can be evangelistic. It shouldn't be optional. But often the smaller church can evangelize best. Your church may not be effective in reaching everyone, so pray about a niche ministry. See whom God lays on your heart. Reach out to that particular group with a new and concentrated effort. If your congregation is getting older, is there a particular way you could focus your efforts on a younger group? It might require change. Many older people who don't like to change for the sake of change, will change for the sake of the mission.

Finding a way to accomplish church renewal often gets complicated. For some churches (the Northwest Church being one of them), all it takes is a single, evangelistic niche ministry.

CHAPTER FIVE

MISSIONS—
MOTIVATING MEMBERS
FOR **GLOBAL EVANGELISM**

DERRICK RITCHIE

I T WAS A PHONE CALL I WAS NOT EXPECTING. The young mother on the other end was ecstatic to tell me some big news. Trying to be excited with her, I asked, "So what is it?" She exclaimed, "I got a job!" This was her first salary job as a teacher, and it would double her family's annual income. "Do you know what this means?" she asked. I was anticipating her to say what several others have told me over the years after a dramatic salary increase—a new car or maybe even a new home. But these were not her words. She said, "This means I can give more money to the church!" As you might guess, this is not the typical response of many church members who call to share news of financial freedom. With all of her excitement about more money, the first thought on her mind was that of helping God's ministry and mission.

This Christian lady's attitude is what we are after in unleashing the potential of the church. We are not so much seeking a strategy or planned program; instead, we are longing to raise up Spirit-filled people in our churches who earnestly desire to live out the greatest commandments of Jesus to the fullest extent—to love God with all they have and share his love with the world.

A few years ago, I read an article by John Piper that altered my outlook on missions. He wrote, "Missions is not the ultimate goal of the church. Worship is. Missions exists because worship doesn't . . . worship, therefore, is the fuel and goal of missions" ("Let The Nations Be Glad!," *Perspectives,* 1999). Our ultimate goal is worship. Our church's mission is fulfilled when we understand the greatness of God and, in our worship of him, cannot help but desire to share him with every human being on earth. In this we are not trying to lay out a program of missions; rather, we are trying to spark an enthusiasm for worship that cannot be contained within the church walls, that overflows to the ends of the earth. When we want everyone on earth to have the great blessing and hope of worshiping our Lord Jesus Christ, this goal of worship propels us into missions.

Our Mission History

The Tower Hill Christian Church is located in central Illinois and has existed for more than one hundred ten years. We average one hundred fifty in attendance on Sunday mornings in our small community of six hundred fifty people. We are blessed also to draw from surrounding communities. Our demographic includes farmers, teachers, factory workers, and several employed outside the area where their drive time to the city is about an hour one way. The church has been blessed to have most of her ministers serve five to ten years. In the mid-1980s, one of those ministers left the preaching ministry at Tower Hill to serve full-time with his wife on the mission field in Africa. This couple receives our largest amount of mission support to this day. Currently we support fifteen different missions, more than half of which are involved in cross-cultural work around the world.

In the mid-1970s, the church's minister cast the vision for a faith promise missions program at Tower Hill. This was no small transition for a congregation that was giving only a small percentage of its annual budget to missions. It seemed that paying the minister and keeping up with other expenses left little room for this smaller church to think seriously about missions. But the minister challenged the people to make yearly pledges that required faith and sacrifice. No longer would the church support missions from a small percentage of the total budget. Instead each year they would pray, set a financial goal as a congregation, and make individual promises to God in faith regarding the amount of money they would give in the coming year to missions. They believed God would enable them to sacrifice and would provide the money so they could fulfill their promises. Today, more than three decades after adopting the faith promise model, our congregation has witnessed tremendous growth in our missions giving. The church consistently gives around 40 percent or more of its annual budget to missions, and has gone from giving a few thousand dollars annually to commitments of more than fifty thousand dollars each year.

Allow me to address some of the blessings that have resulted from our faith promise program—blessing other churches can benefit from as well. I will also highlight some of the challenges presented to a smaller church when it chooses to give substantially to missions.

Mission Adventure Trips

In the mid-1990s we added a new dimension to our faith promise effort—we call it Mission Adventure. This endeavor has reenergized our faith promise program and renewed our desire to support God's global mission.

During the era of the minister who preceded me, our leadership made the decision to designate two hundred dollars a month from our missions giving to a Mission Adventure fund. This fund would be used mainly for mission trip travel expenses and supplies for our missionaries during these trips.

I had never considered such a concept—I had known only of special fundraising activities to support individuals on mission trips. Today our church is richly blessed to have funds readily available when we plan a mission trip. Mission trips unite us in the goal of world evangelism and give us zeal at home in our service to the Lord.

I was fortunate in the first year of my ministry at Tower Hill to go on a mission trip to central Mexico with several leaders in our church. We grew closer, talked more, and dreamed bigger about our ministry in those eight days of traveling than we likely would have in an entire year. That short trip energized us in ministry and mission.

Our Mission Adventure program has allowed us to average almost one major mission trip each year along with several one-day trips to local missions we support. Currently we are planning future trips to our missionaries in Japan and a second trip to Mexico. In the past five years we have made trips to Mexico, Ivory Coast, New England, and the Midwest. These trips were made possible by more than fifteen thousand dollars from the Mission Adventure fund—money set aside for this purpose. In addition, Mission Adventure allows us to purchase supplies used during our mission trips. For example, while in Mexico, we helped lay a concrete floor for a church and were able to contribute more than one thousand dollars toward construction supplies. Mission Adventure has also allowed us to give money to the missionaries at end of each trip for extra expenses incurred while we were there and to give them a financial boost.

With the inauguration of our Mission Adventure program, some in our congregation could not imagine why we would "waste" our money on travel expenses when that money could be sent directly to our missionaries to assist their ministry. Even today, though Mission Adventure is several years old now, this question still occasionally arises. However, it does not come from our missionaries! They are overjoyed that we take the time and effort to visit their work personally. When we took our two-week trip to Ivory Coast, our missionaries expressed that we were their first supporting church group to visit them on the field in their twenty years of work there. Are we really supporting our missionaries if we never go and participate in their work? Real love and accountability come from seeing, touching, and embracing them personally. In turn, this develops a passion within those who go. They come back and tell what they saw. When this happens, those "impersonal" missionary slide shows and PowerPoint® presentations take on new life and meaning. Firsthand stories are told and pictures shared from people within the congregation who have been on the mission field.

Any member of our congregation may go on a mission trip. We believe such trips encourage both missionary and church member to be active in telling others about the God we worship. As an additional bonus, we have begun supporting at least one other missionary whom we never would have supported if we had not personally met him on the mission field as he worked alongside the missionary we were visiting.

It should be mentioned that adults are our target group for mission trips, not youth. Some churches have the idea that mission trips (as well as conferences, camps, and conventions) are mainly youth activities. We strongly disagree! While trips like these may light a fire of passion in young people, I have sadly witnessed some adults at home quickly extinguish any spark the youth have brought back with them. Because of this, our main goal is to send adults. This is to the smaller church's advantage because often we couldn't round up enough youth for mission trips even if we wanted to. The more the adults go, the more immediate the change that takes place within our church. If several adults in our church go on a mission trip and their hearts are changed, the spiritual vitality and generosity they bring back to the church creates an instant impact.

Change at Home

The more a church gets its members involved in missions, the more ministries at home begin to change and grow as well.

If you want change and enthusiasm in your worship service, send your leaders to Africa to encourage the missionaries there. They, in turn, will bring a new perspective in worship back home. More immediately, get them involved in one of the local prison ministries near the church where they not only will worship differently, but will likely get to share their faith in Christ with someone who does not know. A church's worship and direction are deeply affected by its involvement in missions. The goal is not simply to give money to missions, but to get our people out of their religious comfort zones to experience what God is doing in one of our missions, whether an hour away or a continent away.

As emphasized earlier, the key to motivating members for global evangelism is in melting and remolding their hearts so that they hunger to worship God and passionately want others to know and worship him. Every church needs passionate people who understand the calling of God. One potential obstacle for the smaller church is the impact of negativity. If the smaller church can cultivate hearts for global evangelism among its members, that excitement can grow and spread as it did in the first-century church: "They broke bread in their homes and ate together with glad and sincere hearts, praising God and enjoying the favor of all the people. And the Lord added to their number daily those who were being saved" (Acts 2:46, 47).

Let the members of your church know that there's no such thing as their speaking too often or too boldly about the good things God is doing in their lives and in the church. May those on fire for the Lord squelch any talk that would hinder God's ministry. Bold words of joy and encouragement should be the norm when serving an "all things are possible" God. We may be a smaller church, but we happen to serve a really big God!

Missions-minded churches create a cycle of spiritual fervor. When people get excited locally about the mission of God, they want to take that commitment globally. Likewise, when people experience the worldwide workings of God's church, they want to come home and tell everyone about it.

Annual Faith Promise Rally

Each year in the spring, we conduct a three-week faith promise rally. This enables us to promote worldwide evangelism, explain its importance, and encourage our people to support it. We encourage parents to help their kids fill out faith promise cards so they can participate in a lifestyle of giving to God and his mission. We set up displays from as many of our missionaries as possible, and invite a different speaker each week from one of our missions to come and share during our Sunday school hour and preach a missions-focused sermon. On the third Sunday, faith promise cards are collected, we announce our total promises, and we celebrate with a fellowship dinner.

Each year we strive to raise our giving goal. Sometimes this increase is a few hundred dollars; at other times it may be a thousand dollars. We have also found it helpful to list other major church funds on our faith promise commitment cards so the congregation is aware of our total budget needs. While faith promise commitments are made only toward missions, we want to inform everyone and ask them to pray and think about their total giving to God and his mission through our church.

Growth Areas and Challenges

I'll be honest—while giving to missions leads to many spiritual benefits that impact eternity, it also affects our ministry spending at home. I know of several churches about our size that already support a second full-time minister; we are not yet able to commit to another full-time salary because of the amount we give to missions. Currently, we have a part-time youth minister with hopes of supporting someone full-time within a year or two.

We need to be careful about how we view this matter. It might be easy to claim this sacrifice at home to be some sort of spiritual calling to suffer while supporting the kingdom worldwide. This line of reasoning, I believe, is faulty. We do no favors to our missionaries if we allow our church at home to stagnate or die because we do not have the funds to reach out to our local kids and families, pay the minister a livable wage, and serve the congregation at home, keeping it healthy and growing.

The other extreme is to be avoided as well. It may also be easy for a church to become focused on itself in such a way that it neglects the Great Commission. A well-balanced spiritual plan of local and worldwide ministry is essential. We aim to walk the line in which the mission of our church is equally divided between the mission at home and the mission to the ends of the earth. A synergy takes place when a congregation sacrificially supports and is involved heavily in both areas. We have seen it at Tower Hill in the many ways God has blessed and grown our ministry. Yet we continue to ask God's guidance concerning our mission locally so we can support the kingdom globally. Our goal is vibrant ministry here that leads to effective ministry there.

Other churches face a similar struggle, trying to maintain the balance God desires for his church in accomplishing the mission, both at home and worldwide. But if we step out in faith and participate more in missions, that desired balance will come to the church. Several action steps have helped us unleash our potential in global evangelism.

Unleashing Your Mission Potential

Visit missionaries on the field. Our goal is to visit by 2010 the field of every missionary we support. We want to encourage them, recognize their needs, maintain accountability, and get to know them personally as we work together for the cause of Christ. As a tip for gaining momentum, the next time missionaries come to your church to give a presentation, ask them during a question and answer time what it would mean to them if your church sent a group to see their work and meet them on the field. They will let everyone know it would be no waste of money.

Set aside money for mission trips. We never hold special fundraisers for a trip because the money is already set aside in our budget. Every church can decide on some level to designate funds for mission trips. Let the money accumulate, and your biggest hurdle will already have been cleared when plans are made for a trip.

Schedule an annual time of missions challenge. We spend at least three Sundays each year challenging our people with their giving and reminding them who our missionaries are and of their need for our support. Make it an annual priority to challenge your people in their giving and participation in missions. We pay an honorarium to our speakers and cover their expenses so they can come, share, challenge, and let us to get to know them and better understand their ministry.

Get involved with local missions. Not every mission trip has to be expensive and lengthy. We have been blessed by becoming more involved with an inner-city mission and a prison ministry a few hours away. While the major trips are affordable once a year at most, we can stay involved by working with local missions several times each year. These local trips can bring great spiritual change to those who attend and build long-term relationships with the mission.

Think of your missionaries as family. We know several of our missionaries very well. They need no introduction when they come to our church. They have become more than just names to whom we send money; they are an intricate part of our ministry and fellowship. We strive to care for them as we do any other family in our congregation. While we may not be able to know all our missionaries on this level, it is a blessing to our ministry and theirs for us to have a close relationship.

Giving the Best We Have

I have heard stories about missionaries being viewed as second-class citizens or as people who were not able to make it in the American church. One of our missionaries once received a package of used tea bags from someone. Apparently this giver's church had taught a philosophy about missionaries: "They get our leftovers."

What does your church teach about the importance of missionaries and their work? Do you emphasize that they go because they have a special calling and purpose from God to share the message of his Son to a hurting world? Everyone deserves to know and worship the Lord Jesus Christ as we do. Our missionaries are out to accomplish this mission. They are gifted servants who have made incredible sacrifices in order to spread the message of God's love. May our churches begin to give quality, sacrificial support so that they can do their work most productively. They deserve much more than leftovers!

CHAPTER SIX

WORSHIP—
PERMEATING THE LIFE OF THE CHURCH
DAN HARGRAVE

N THE RURAL CHURCH THAT WAS MY FIRST FULL-TIME MINISTRY, WE WERE BLESSED WITH A NUMBER OF PIANISTS AND ORGANISTS. It was a rare commodity for such a small congregation. Two of the women had played for years, and it was their preference to be scheduled together. Nearly every time their rotation came around, however, the song leader would announce the next hymn and the ladies would begin playing different songs! The song leader would chuckle, "I don't care which one you play, ladies. Just pick one!"

Many smaller churches overlook the importance of doing worship well. Someone grabs a hymnal and picks out three songs. If there are a few younger folks around, they might throw in a chorus or two. There is no real plan—it is just something that needs to be done to get to Communion and the sermon. Ministers scold Sunday school and Bible class leaders for waiting until Saturday night to prepare. Yet many church leaders do the same thing when it comes to preparing for the worship service. The end result is a dull, disconnected, and disappointing exercise of spiritual gymnastics.

The great devotional writer Oswald Chambers observed, "Worship is giving God the best that he has given you. Be careful what you do with the best you have. Whenever you get a blessing from God, give it back to him as a love-gift . . . offer the blessing back to him in a deliberate act of worship." We should take seriously Chambers's words, no matter the size of our congregation. Every part of our worship experience, which goes far beyond the worship service, must include giving back God's best that he has given us. To approach a worship service without serious planning is to sully God's best by our inattention and carelessness. Worship that will make a difference in the life of our congregations demands our best efforts.

King David offered this prayer of worship: "To you, O GOD belong the greatness and the might, the glory, the victory, the majesty, the splendor; Yes! Everything in heaven, everything on earth; the kingdom all yours! You've raised yourself high over all" (1 Chronicles 29:11, *The Message*). Like David, we want the worship at Stokelan Drive Christian Church to reflect our commitment to directing all the credit and glory to God. It is our intention that all facets of our worship, from the announcements to the closing chorus, focus on delivering that Sunday's message. We want our congregation to take a life-changing truth home with them each week. We are still a work in progress, but let me share with you how we have arrived at where we are and what we intend to do to remain on this path of life-changing worship.

Our Community

The city of Malden is located at the top of the Bootheel region of southeastern Missouri. It is situated in the heart of the region's cotton belt. With a population of about five thousand people, Malden is a racially diverse, mid- to lower-income community. The citizens of Malden are proud of their southern heritage and history. An Army air base was located in Malden during the Korean War era. Many servicemen made their way to Malden for training, and the city seeks to preserve this part of its history. Although agriculture drives the local economy, there are also many manufacturing jobs within a thirty-mile radius. Still, many people live on government assistance.

Malden calls itself the Hub City because it is at the center of several smaller communities. Many of the residents of these communities come to Malden to shop, to receive primary medical attention, and to attend church. Most of these churches are traditional, small-town churches and fit the definition of a smaller church.

Our Congregation

Stokelan Drive Christian Church seeks to be "A Place of Ministry: Reaching God—Touching Lives." This simple mission statement directs our ministries and programs. The church celebrated her twenty-fifth anniversary in 2004 and has seen consistent growth since 2000. Between 2000–2004, the average attendance of the congregation grew by more than 40 percent. It is a congregation made up of a wide spectrum of age groups, religious backgrounds, and economic resources. The people who make up SDCC are a warm and friendly group. We often joke that if you leave the building without a hug, it's your own fault. The congregation has developed a sense of inclusiveness that allows newcomers to feel like a part of the group. One of our newer families commented to me that a determining factor in their decision to join the congregation was the "sameness" with which everyone is treated. No matter who you are or what you have, you will be treated equally at Stokelan Drive Christian Church.

Our Story

In the late 1990s, several of our church members began taking notice of the "graying" of our congregation. In fact, some of our younger adults were in their late thirties and early forties. With the recognition that the congregation was growing older came the realization that unless we actively sought to reach younger people, we would face the inevitable demise of our church. Individually and congregationally, we began to pray, "Lord, send us some younger people." Soon, a few younger families began arriving at our door. I am ashamed to admit that we were almost surprised by this development because we had not planned what we would do when God answered our prayers.

A family who began attending was looking for a place to minister and possessed a great deal of musical ability. I told our leaders that since God had honored our prayers, we had the responsibility to use the people he had sent. We began to sing a few more praise choruses accompanied by guitar and bass on Sunday evenings. Eventually we added a few extra singers. Finally, we tried it on a Sunday morning. The response was pretty good. Most people enjoyed this change, although some expressed reservations. Usually, my response was to remind them that they had prayed for new people; and since God had sent them, we needed to do what it took to keep them! It is hard for someone to argue with you when you remind them that God has answered their prayers!

A biblical principle began taking shape in our congregation. Jesus said, "Neither do men pour new wine into old wineskins. If they do, the skins will burst, the wine will run out and the wineskins will be ruined. No, they pour new wine into new wineskins, and both are preserved" (Matthew 9:17). In our midst, there was a sense that God was discarding some of the old wineskins we had used for years and was now giving us new wineskins that would carry his work into the future. And it seemed that the more we opened ourselves up to these new wineskins, the more new people began attending.

Certain dangers become evident when change leads to success. Success whispers in your ear, "If this change worked, then everything will work. So go ahead and do whatever you want." There's the danger of taking shortcuts, bypassing the needed work that changes demand. There is also the danger of insensitivity toward those who do not want things to be different from what they have known. Another danger comes when you focus so much on retaining your new members that you forget to minister to your long-standing members. None of these dangers have to defeat you. In fact, if you are aware of their presence, they can become warning flags that may actually help you accomplish your goal.

A cartoon in my files pictures a preacher standing behind a pulpit with a distressed look on his face. The caption reads, "Somewhere between point one and point two, the preacher realized that point three misses the point altogether." In our efforts to make our worship more relevant and life-changing, we have missed the point at times. To get back on track, we remember our goal of "Reaching God and Touching Lives." We evaluate the components in our services by asking, "Is this helping people connect with God and giving them an opportunity for a life change?" This drives us to make several decisions about our worship services.

First, we want to present a message that is contemporary and relevant. Therefore, we want to plan every part of our service around one theme. Since I mostly preach sermon series, we are able to plan several weeks in advance. We ask those who are doing Communion meditations and special music to base their selections on the weekly theme. To help those who are responsible for the music, we will from time to time assign a song that fits with a given week's theme.

Second, we do not want to totally abandon our long-held worship traditions. Since we currently have only one morning service, we have combined both newer and older components in it. We use hymns as well as contemporary songs. We sing songs with a full band, some with piano and organ, and some a cappella.

Third, the Lord's Supper remains a focal point of our worship services, and we use a variety of methods to present it. Most weeks, Communion is celebrated in the middle of the service. But there are times when we choose to move it to a different place in the service to better present that week's theme. We give those who are doing the meditation the freedom to be creative in their presentation. Some will use video or other forms of media to lead us to the Lord's table.

Fourth, we continue to emphasize the preached Word, believing that when "we preach Christ crucified" (1 Corinthians 1:23) lives are changed. Nevertheless, we now preach the Word using drama and video as well as the Sunday sermon. We incorporate PowerPoint® presentations to help reinforce the message. I typically preach in a conversational style and invite audience participation in the message. We also use props and take-homes to enhance the delivery of the message. When we developed the theme "Building a Great Church," everyone received a replica construction helmet labeled with each week's theme. The first Sunday of this campaign, it looked as if we had been invaded by a bizarre Bob the Builder cult! Yet it became a very effective device to reinforce the message.

Fifth, we have tapped into the creative gifts of our members to help us present the message. During our "Building a Great Church" campaign, our decorating team built a miniature church building in our lobby. One Sunday during the construction of this building, members were encouraged to write their names on the structure as a way of reinforcing the truth that people make up the church.

One might question what this has to do with worship. Since worship involves giving God the best he has given you, then we must do whatever we can so that each member can give his best, no matter what it is. Worship cannot permeate the life of the church if it does not connect with all believers on levels where they can give their best.

Challenges We Have Faced

The process of being authentic in our worship is an ongoing struggle. One of the most common challenges we face comes from those who fall into the "we like the old way" camp. We'll always have some people who long for the old days. Each of us has happy memories of days gone by, but when faced with the prospect of actually reliving them, most of us would decline. I try to convince the questioner that we are trying to be true to the traditions of our congregation without being hampered by them. I remind objectors that our outreach has grown significantly since we became more progressive in our worship. I also remind them that our Sunday evening services remain very much traditional, even old-timey. If that does not work, I'll humbly tell them that we have prayerfully made the decision to move in this new direction and ask that they be patient with us as we seek to follow the Lord's leading.

Another challenge has come from those who think the music is too loud. Sometimes they are right! It is difficult to find a volume level that is pleasing to everyone. When this issue is brought to me, I explain that we are working hard by means of additional practice and equipment not to offend anyone. I ask for patience as we do our best to lead a worship service that will be a blessing to everyone.

A third challenge falls into the category of personal preference. From time to time, I'll have a church member tell me that he just doesn't like a particular song, or that band members should dress up for church, or that we should use hymnals instead of projecting the words on a screen. I usually deflect this challenge by admitting that I don't necessarily like everything we do either. We are a diverse group of people, so we all must give and take a little. As a gentle nudge away from the selfishness in this challenge, I remind the member that we aren't really doing this for us anyway. Our worship is for God first.

The Result

I suppose some would classify our worship style as blended, but we prefer to think of it solely as "our style." It is what fits our situation. We are doing what we can to help our congregation—young and old, new believer and old saint—to connect with God in a way that fits. Some of our members stand with their hands raised. Others remain seated with their heads bowed. Some clap their hands while others shout "Amen!" Tears of gratitude flow, and joy-filled laughter fills the room. And there is a great deal of fun . . . the kind of fun that only happens when you are celebrating the presence of the Lord. And best of all, we have grown by an additional 26 percent in our morning worship service during the past year.

The Future

People enter our building to worship with expressions that say, *I wonder what they are going to do next!* As leaders in the church, it is our job to foster that sense of anticipation. We need to build a spirit of expectancy for what God is going to accomplish here. To that end, we are working several plans for the immediate and long-range future.

We plan to become a more event-oriented congregation. My daughter Amy is the marketing director for a mortgage firm in Nashville. She told me that her company wants to have an in-home contact with potential customers between six and eight times a year. They do this using a variety of creative methods. We can apply that mentality to our community, giving our citizens at least that many opportunities to consider the ministry and outreach of Stokelan Drive Christian Church. If we can get someone to visit us at least once, we have the potential to lead him or her into a personal relationship with the Lord. Recently we hosted an outdoor gospel concert and cookout. The music and food were free to all who attended, and several new contacts were made.

We also plan for more seating in our worship center. We have not decided on whether to add more services, to expand our seating in our current facility, or to build a bigger building. We are trusting that the Lord will lead our master planning team in the way we need to go.

A third plan is to tweak the service to keep it fresh. It is easy to find a comfort zone and just keep doing the same thing. But this gives the congregation an opportunity to go on autopilot and lose connection with the worship service. Our worship of almighty God demands our very best!

Advice

Much damage is done when a congregation becomes a battleground in the worship wars. One would think that meaningful Christian worship would not be so difficult to accomplish. If changes to your worship service seem impossible, don't give up. Make sure your motives are sincere and the project is worth doing; then stick with it. Here are a few thoughts I have found to be helpful in the development of our worship ministry.

• Go slow. Let me repeat that because it is so important—Go slow. I know that may not be what we want to hear. We want to whip our congregations into shape overnight. Years ago, my dad gave me some great advice that he had learned in his years of ministry. He told me, "Son, the people were there before you came to that church and they'll be there after you are gone." In other words, we need to learn to work with our leaders and congregation rather than in competition with them.

We may want to go within a week's time from a service where the most contemporary song is "Rock of Ages" to a service that features a full band and light show and a preacher delivering the sermon in khaki shorts and a polo shirt. We may be right about needing to change what happens in our worship services, but shoving it down the throats of the congregation will not achieve the desired results. We have taken the steps of change incrementally, allowing the congregation to get on board.

• Know your audience. Plan your worship with sensitivity to the demographics of your congregation. Some of the components we use in our worship service for teens would not work well on Sunday morning. When we first started making some changes in our worship service, I would say to our young guitarist, "Andy, you have got to know the audience." To my great pleasure, I heard him say the same thing recently to our new teenage drummer. This is true in the selection of music, dramas, video clips, and sermon themes. It is a comfort zone issue for most of us. We like to do what we like to do. Yet when we recognize that worship isn't about us, we begin to shape our choices based on the criteria of glorifying God and meeting the needs of the congregation.

• Work on your transitions. Transitions are those moments that take place as you go from one segment of your service to another. Smaller churches are notorious for dead air, similar to that noticeable glitch on your television when a commercial or program does not begin on time. You get a blue screen and the sense that someone messed up. Dead air gives the viewer time to punch the button on the remote control and switch to another program. A "blue screen" in our services can cause the congregation to mentally change channels. Although it takes extra effort, I believe we need to work on the production of our worship services so that worship leaders are where they are supposed to be when they are supposed to be there.

We ask everyone who is going to be on the platform during the service to sit in the front rows so that we don't have to wait on them to get to the stage. If we make the worshipers wait on us, we are inviting them to turn their attention elsewhere. This is an ongoing process for our church. We still have some people who simply don't want to move out of their favorite place to sit, even for one Sunday. We are trying to encourage and educate these folks about the need to eliminate dead air.

Action Steps

Perhaps you have been challenged to rethink your approach to worship, but the task seems so big you don't know where to begin. Let me offer a few practical solutions. This list is far from exhaustive, but these things have worked for us.

• **Work with what you've got.** This is one of my favorite mantras for our worship team. It is easy to fall into the trap of saying, "If only we had a guitarist or a drummer or computer whiz or an award-winning actor or a larger budget, we could have a great worship service." Yet God has taught us that when we take what we have and offer it back to him, he is able to do amazing things. Remember what he did with a few loaves of bread and a couple of fish.

• **Be on the lookout for potential servants in your worship ministry.** It takes a little work to uncover the hidden talents in your congregation, especially if you have new people attending your services. Our tendency often is to involve the same people over and over again. We must take the time to look for new participants and cultivate their abilities. Listen to the other members of your team—they often are more aware of the talents and abilities of your congregation than you are.

• **Embrace technology.** I grew up with flannelgraph lessons in Sunday school, but today's children are unimpressed by this approach. On the other hand, show them a quick-moving video clip and you'll have their attention. Why should we think their parents are any different? Members of your congregation are on the lookout for new technologies in the computer, television, and audio systems they use at home and work. In this day of high-definition television, wireless Internet, and cell phones with more features than you could possibly use, our worship services must have a technology-friendly mindset.

When we first discussed purchasing a video projector and screen, some of our leaders were skeptical. Now even the most skeptical of these leaders think of creative ways we can use technology to accomplish our goal of reaching people for Christ. It is not necessary to invest thousands of dollars in technology in order to achieve the benefits of it. Start simply and slowly, building your system as your needs and resources increase. If you encounter resistance from your leaders, ask them to do business for a week without their telephones and computers. If they would not want to do that, ask them if the Lord's work is unimportant enough to do without the best tools available.

Our Best Efforts

No church, regardless of its size, can afford to be casual in the matter of worshiping the God of all creation. Effective worship is not dependent on the size of the church; rather, effective worship is a reflection of the heart of a church. Furthermore, relevant worship is a great weapon in the spiritual warfare to which we all have been called. Jim Cymbala, in his book *Fresh Wind, Fresh Fire* (Zondervan, 1997) writes, "The truth of the matter is that the devil is not terribly frightened of our human efforts and credentials. But he knows his kingdom will be damaged when we lift up our hearts to God."

May we all commit ourselves to giving worship our best effort. It is the only reasonable response to the very best that God has given us.

CHAPTER SEVEN

FAMILY MINISTRY—
HELPING PARENTS DISCIPLE THEIR CHILDREN

DAVID LANGFORD

THE QUAKER AVENUE CHURCH OF CHRIST IS IN LUBBOCK, TEXAS, A GROWING COMMUNITY OF TWO HUNDRED THOUSAND. Located in the heart of the farming communities of the South Plains, Lubbock also hosts a large public university (Texas Tech University), a smaller Christian university (Lubbock Christian University), as well as satellite campuses of South Plains Junior College and Wayland Baptist University. Lubbock also serves as a medical center for the region with three major hospitals. Though a city of churches, the state university presents also a secular influence in the community. Lubbock has a diverse population with an especially strong Hispanic heritage (29 percent of the population).

The Quaker Avenue church was established in 1945 and has an average attendance of three hundred on Sunday mornings. There are several congregations of the Churches of Christ in Lubbock, five having memberships of one thousand or more. Quaker Avenue is served by nine elders, fourteen deacons, two full-time ministers, and two part-time staff. The church is an unusually age-integrated church with almost equal numbers of members represented in each ten-year interval from zero to one hundred. Quaker belongs to churches known for not using Sunday schools, but is nonsectarian and enthusiastically seeks to participate with churches of all traditions whenever possible.

Several years ago I received a call from a Christian brother who had been an education minister here in Lubbock at one of the larger churches. He had taken a new ministry in another state. The church he now worked with was dissatisfied with their traditional approach to education and youth ministry; they were looking for a different model, one that would more effectively integrate their members and focus more on families and the teaching role of parents. On the phone John told me that in one of their staff meetings, they were discussing what a different model might look like, and he suddenly remembered the little church in Lubbock that didn't have Sunday school. So he called and asked what we did to teach our families—what was our alternative to Sunday school? He hoped to find a well-thought-out educational model that focused on the family and created a greater sense of community in the church.

It was true that our church did not use the Sunday school educational model. It was also true that our congregation enjoyed a strong sense of community with rich intergenerational relationships. Visitors often commented on that. But as far as having a well-thought-out model of education, there wasn't much to offer John. I shared a few of our programs and activities that I thought might help, but after the conversation ended I felt convicted. More thought should go into designing an educational model that reflected the values of our distinct heritage, a heritage that in its rhetoric had argued that the family was the primary classroom and parents the best teachers of children, but in practice had been less faithful in actually helping parents fulfill that calling. That conversation began a process that continues today, the goal of which is to develop a discipling method that empowers parents to teach their children in a church environment that supports the home as the child's best classroom.

A Family-Oriented Church

The phrase *a family-oriented church* is common on church signs everywhere. But often the larger a church becomes, the more difficult it is for families to do much together. Family members are typically separated into different classes, ministries, and sometimes even different worship services. As various subgroups become larger in a church (children, teens, singles, seniors, and so on), pressure grows to subdivide ministry, providing each group with its own minister and set of activities. Such an approach to ministry can provide many blessings, for each of these subgroups has particular needs that can often be better met in more specialized ministry. But this approach is not without its negative consequences as well—not the least of which can be a de-emphasis on the role of parents in the spiritual discipling of their children and a loss of the sense of community within the church. The difference is not unlike the difference between the suburban mall of the city and the town square of the smaller village. Both are places to gather and shop. In the mall a crowd of people, not very familiar with one another, gather and move by each other seeking specialty stores in which they want to shop. In the town square shopping is more limited, but it is also less important than the opportunity to meet good friends and visit around the square. The strength of the large church is its multiple ministries. The strength of the smaller church is its greater sense of community.

At Quaker, we are more of a town-square church. One way we have sought to maximize our strengths has been to nurture our family orientation by developing a family discipling program that would encourage parents in their role as spiritual mentors to their children and also enable our church community to be more involved in the faith development of our young people. A family discipling ministry is of particular value to smaller churches because a program like this does not require the resources of multiple ministers. Rather, the goal is to empower parents and maximize the natural learning environment of the family.

The Discipling Role of Parents

Christian parents and church leaders understand the importance of the involvement of parents in the spiritual discipleship of their children. We're familiar with the classic passages in Deuteronomy 6 and Ephesians 6. But obeying those commands has become more challenging for today's parents. Parent involvement in children's development is increasingly marginalized by the expanding agenda of public education. Parents are expected to send their children to school at earlier ages. The school day and the school year are longer. Schools have our children for most of the day, most of the week, most of the year, for most of their early lives. The time children can spend with parents is substantially eroded. The scriptural admonition to teach our children when we sit at home, walk along the road, lie down at night, and get up in the morning is no small challenge when our children have practices and rehearsals before and after school, homework when they finally do get home, and are considered truant if they take too many days out to sit down or walk along with their parents.

At the same time, parents' confidence in their ability to train their children is shaken by the new culture of marriage and family "experts" whose specialized education in areas traditionally taught by parents is considerably more than the average mom's or dad's. Schools today provide more instruction on topics once seen as more appropriate to the home. The need for such education in our schools has been brought about by the increasing diversity of our communities. Yet, it is that very diversity in our culture that argues most for greater parental involvement with children. Public schools are not the ideal place for our children to receive education about matters for which our faith provides the best answers.

The recent emergence of the home-school movement is one indication that many parents are seeing the need to be more personally involved in the education of their children. In fact, the growing popularity of the home-school model is creating pressure not only on schools but also on churches to develop educational models that similarly encourage parents to become more involved in their child's faith development. Most churches use teaching programs that follow the public school model of age segregated classes. The family discipling program we have been developing at Quaker Avenue more resembles the home school-model with its emphasis on parents and the value of intergenerational relationships.

Designing *Faith Chronicles:* The Theory

Most parents desire to be more involved in their children's spiritual training, but often become discouraged at their lack of success in maintaining a regular plan of Bible study. The three primary problems parents identify that explain their lack of success in having consistent and effective family Bible study are: (1) a lack of time, (2) a lack of Bible knowledge, and (3) a lack of ability to teach.

In designing *Faith Chronicles* I wanted to create a program that did not seem overwhelming and that any parent would feel capable of leading. First, it needed to be flexible enough to fit any schedule so that families can begin with a modest time commitment. I assured parents that even a thirty-minute devotional together once a week can make a significant impact on children. The secret to effective family devotionals has less to do with the total amount of time spent and everything to do with commitment to a regular time.

Perhaps even more frustrating in the minds of many parents is their concern that they have an inadequate knowledge of the Bible. I have found, however, that people often have more Bible knowledge than they give themselves credit for. For example, most parents are familiar with several of the classic Bible stories, and that familiarity provides a larger reservoir of Bible knowledge than they realize. Our second emphasis in the design was to focus the content on those classic Bible stories. As parents and children discuss these stories, the parents' latent Bible knowledge becomes a resource. And for those parents whose knowledge of Bible stories is more limited, reading these stories along with their children is a great way to develop their own Bible knowledge. Parents are encouraged to follow a very simple devotional plan with their children:

Tell the story. Parents begin by telling the stories to their children with the expectation that children will eventually learn to tell the stories themselves.

Place the story in its chronology. Equally important to knowing the story is knowing how each story fits into the larger drama of the Bible.

Learn the memory verse. Each story includes a Scripture which captures a key spiritual principle taught in the story.

Keep a journal. As parent-child discussions reveal the spiritual insights learned from these stories, children are encouraged to keep a journal and chronicle their own faith development.

Finally I want to help parents discover that they are, by nature, the best teachers their children can have. Moses instructed the parents of Israel to teach their children "when you sit at home and when you walk along the road, when you lie down and when you get up" (Deuteronomy 6:7). The implication of that verse is that faith is best taught in the daily routines and relationships of the home as children witness both the words and the works of the people they live with. Historically, "the faith" has been passed down from one generation to the next by the simple act of parents telling their children the great stories of the Bible. The theme passage selected for the *Faith Chronicles* curriculum comes from Psalm 78.

> O my people, hear my teaching; listen to the words of my mouth.
> I will open my mouth in parables,
> I will utter hidden things, things from of old—
> what we have heard and known, what our fathers have told us.
> We will not hide them from their children; we will tell the next generation
> the praiseworthy deeds of the LORD, his power, and the wonders he
>   has done. . . .
> So the next generation would know them, even the children yet to be born,
> and they in turn would tell their children. Then they would put their trust
>   in God
> and would not forget his deeds but would keep his commands.
>
> PSALM 78:1-4, 6, 7

My hope for *Faith Chronicles* is to inspire parents to teach their children the praiseworthy deeds of the Lord so they will put their trust in the Lord and continue that legacy of faith by teaching their own children.

Making *Faith Chronicles* Intergenerational

To further encourage families to accept their discipling responsibility, it was important that our church environment support parents in their task and affirm the children's faith development. As is often quoted, "It takes a village to raise a child." Our congregations must be spiritual villages, communities of faith that nurture in our children a sense of belonging to the larger church family. At Quaker we conscientiously plan our fellowship and ministries in such a way that by the time our children graduate from high school, they will include among their closest relationships not only their peers, but many other church members as well. To facilitate that, some components in the *Faith Chronicles* plan were designed to encourage greater intergenerational relationships.

Elder Visits in the Home

As families sign up to participate in *Faith Chronicles*, our elders and their wives are scheduled to visit and participate in one of the family study times. Sometimes children are encouraged to share a memory verse or perhaps tell the story for the night. Other times the elder is invited to be the guest storyteller. In any case, such visits give an opportunity for our elders to encourage parents in their discipling role and emphasize to the children the importance of what their parents are doing. Such visits also present a wonderful opportunity for the elders to offer prayers of blessing for the children and the family.

Public Storytelling

During several of our Wednesday services, we give our younger children opportunities to tell a Bible story to the congregation. I have been amazed at the ability of even our youngest children to remember and tell these stories, proving again how powerful story is as a teaching device. In addition to the younger children telling the story to the church, the older ones prepare a lesson for the congregation based on the three questions provided in their journals: (1) What does this story tell us about God? (2) What does this story tell us about man? (3) What does it tell us about how we should live in this world? This simple template of three questions has provided an effective tool to develop the public teaching abilities of our young people.

Family Banquet

Periodically a special banquet hosted by our elders is planned to honor each family participating in *Faith Chronicles*. A special guest speaker is usually invited. The most moving experience of the night is always the parent testimonies. The parents are asked to tell why it is important that their children know God. Particularly inspiring are the words of many fathers who have never spoken publicly in the church, but who, on this occasion, are amazingly eloquent. Seeing their parents' loving and sometimes tearful declarations of faith has a profound impact on these children.

Implementing *Faith Chronicles*

In most churches, implementing a family-based discipling program will be a challenge because the educational program already in place was not designed with the goal of family discipleship. In such cases it is probably wiser to offer a more family-oriented model as an option alongside the more traditional model. It may be that only a few families are interested, but starting a new program with a few families may make it easier to discover and solve unexpected problems.

At Quaker Avenue we didn't have this problem because our church belongs to a tradition that rejected the Sunday school model of teaching. When Sunday schools first became popular in the early 1900s, our spiritual forefathers rejected them as unauthorized by the New Testament and as potentially undermining the role of parents in teaching their children. Since those early years our congregations have become less sectarian about the issue, but they have generally not used the Sunday school method. Consequently, most of our members grew up in churches with no systematic educational method. Though we preached the importance of parents teaching their children, we didn't do much to help them to do it. The challenge for us at Quaker was to become more systematic and accountable for something that had previously been idiosyncratic and private. Sunday school participation is expected in churches that use that model. My goal is that we will develop the same expectation of participation in our family discipleship program.

As mentioned earlier, part of the resistance to family discipleship is a culture in which public schools have gradually assumed from parents many of their traditional teaching responsibilities. Churches have taken their cues from the public education model, sorting children into various age-segregated classes. The message sent, however unintended, is that children are best taught by professionals. Mature and dedicated parents will teach their children regardless of the culture, but less mature parents and those without examples of parents as spiritual mentors may sometimes be encouraged to rely too much on the church and school to teach their children. The emergence of the home-school culture is changing expectations of parents today in dramatic ways.

In the early days of the movement, homeschoolers and public educators were often adversarial and confrontational. Some parents, for that reason, were not attracted to the idea of homeschooling. However, in recent years the practice has become more common as have many other educational models that facilitate greater parental involvement in children's education. In our own congregation the enthusiasm for a family discipleship model has grown among our younger parents in recent years. Churches should take advantage of this trend and adapt their programs to facilitate this desire in parents.

Future Plans

After using *Faith Chronicles* for several years, there is a need to revitalize the model as it becomes routine over time. Some developments that have created new interest are worth sharing.

Faith Workshops for Families

Parents often ask advice about what to do when their children start expressing a desire to be baptized. They are excited, but they are unsure about how old a child should be to take such an important step. Many traditions provide confirmation or preparation classes for children. We decided to develop a more family-oriented approach: a faith workshop for families. The workshop is simply a series of activities for parents and children to experience together, designed especially to assist parents in sharing their faith with their children. While I facilitate the workshop, parents do most of the actual teaching. The goal is to let these initial inquiries of our children become the impetus for special teaching moments between parent and child. The result may or may not be a decision for baptism, but the workshop does provide opportunity to reinforce the parent-child discipling relationship.

Church Devotional

Another project has been to assign to several of our young people the task of writing a devotional based on one of the stories in the *Faith Chronicles.* Answering the three journal questions forms the outline. These devotionals will be compiled and distributed to our members and others as a daily devotional guide. In this way our young people will be teaching us, adding to their sense of belonging and importance to the body of Christ. The project has generated new excitement among our children and adults. As our children mature in the faith, they are able to see how much they have learned from the stories and are now able to share with others.

Patchwork Families

Another planned project is to set aside some Wednesday night services for intergenerational small groups using *Faith Chronicles.* Following the same format as families follow in the home, these small groups become "patchwork families," sharing and doing activities together at the church. Often in small group ministry the great challenge is how or whether to include children. Usually they are led away to have their own worship time together. Patchwork families, however, would be centered on the children, led by the parents, and supported by other members of the congregation. Each group member, whether a high school or college student, a young single professional, or an elderly widow, works together to help children in the group learn these great stories. In the process, great relationships are formed across the generations.

We believe this new model will also assist us in being more evangelistic to families in our communities. By inviting them to take part in patchwork families, we offer them the opportunity to be more active in teaching their children in a nonthreatening way. Our families can invite other families they know to participate and receive training in this vital parental role.

Building on Your Strengths

Churches minister best when they minister out of their unique strengths. One of the obvious strengths of larger churches is the greater resources available to them. Smaller churches have greater opportunity to develop community. There is a place in the kingdom for both. However, whether in larger or smaller churches, the discipling role of parents is important. It is wise to evaluate our teaching program and ask two questions: (1) Does our current model of education encourage our parents to be more involved or less involved in teaching their children? And (2) Do our various ministries have the effect of creating more community among our members, and especially across the ages, or fragmenting them into various age and interest groups? Smaller churches should not take for granted the natural community of faith they may enjoy, but should build on it. On the other hand, larger churches might devote some of their resources to developing greater parental involvement in the discipling of their children, balancing their other ministries designed to develop the faith of children. It is my hope that the sharing of our experience at Quaker Avenue will encourage more parental involvement and an even greater sense of community in your congregation.

To learn more about *Faith Chronicles*, contact David Langford at dlangford @quakeravenue.com.

CHAPTER EIGHT

CHILDREN'S MINISTRY—
BUILDING A FIRM FOUNDATION

KEN AND SHELLEY GREENE

WHY DO WE HAVE TO GO TO THAT PUNY CHURCH?" our daughter asked as we drove to the church that eventually called us to serve on staff. As the parents of four daughters, we wanted to be involved in a church that we could minister to, and one that could also meet the needs of our family.

Having been involved at a church across town with more than three hundred kids in their children's ministries, we knew what it was like to have multiple programs and opportunities available to our daughters. Could this "puny" church (as our ten-year-old so eloquently put it) with only ten kids be a place where we could be satisfied?

Children's ministry is a big part of our lives. It is, in some way, what brought us to Minnesota. I was called to Crossroads College (then Minnesota Bible College) to teach in the area of youth and family studies. My wife Shelley also had an interest in this area, having been involved in children's ministries for several years at our previous church.

I moved to Minnesota several months before the rest of the family to begin the college year, find a place to live, and look for a new church home. The Marion Church of Christ was the first congregation I visited when I arrived in town. Upon visiting the church, I was impressed with its friendliness, but the facility was somewhat off the beaten path and looked quite dated. But what really prevented me from considering this congregation as a possible church home for our family was that they had seemingly little to offer in the area of children's ministry.

The church had a small, unstaffed nursery room downstairs. The only children I noticed, and there were few, sat with their parents during the services. The church offered Sunday school and VBS programs, but the teachers nearly outnumbered the students. With our background and love for children's ministry, I could see the church's need and struggle. But that need, heightened by the friendliness and nostalgic appeal of a country church, could not compensate for what I saw as our primary responsibility: the spiritual development of our daughters.

It is ironic that what caused me in the beginning to overlook the congregation as a possibility for our new church home would be what would lead Shelley and me back there to minister to that congregation six years later.

The Church Is . . . Where?

The Marion Church of Christ is located in a small township less than eleven miles from Rochester, Minnesota, a city of more than ninety thousand. The congregation has a rich history. The February 19, 1914 edition of the *Minnesota Christian* notes,

> "The entire congregational body of the Church of Christ in Minnesota may well arise and make its profoundest bow to the church in Minneapolis? St. Paul? Duluth? No, the church at Marion, the little country church near Rochester. Here the Restoration Plea was first proclaimed to the people of the state."

Rochester is probably best known for the Mayo Clinic, but before this medical metropolis began, the first services of the Marion Church of Christ were held in the home of a nearby farmer in 1855. At the time the community had several stores, hotels, and saloons, and was contending for the county seat.

Today Marion has a gas station, two motorcycle shops, a campground, a cemetery, and an auto-recycling center. The congregation that was once made up of area farmers is now largely professional. The city of Rochester is quickly approaching this outlying area as farmland is developed into upper middle-class housing. The congregation currently averages about one hundred on Sunday mornings.

This congregation has a proud heritage and is attempting to create a productive future for God's kingdom as well. The church has updated its facility to attract new families but struggles with space, accessibility, and visibility issues. Currently we are seeking God's guidance to purchase property in an area more visible to traffic and on land that could offer opportunities for additional ministries to allow spiritual and numerical growth.

How Did We Get Here?

I agreed to become the interim minister to this congregation in early 2003. For several years, the church's vision had been inwardly focused, and they were in a period of decline. At the time, the church was averaging around seventy.

My plan was to fill the pulpit until a new minister could be located. But God had other plans. I fell in love with the people of this church who desired to discover a way to thrive and minister more effectively. Often when I preached, I brought one of our daughters with me, while Shelley continued at her ministry. The girls enjoyed the individual attention in their classes and getting to know their teachers on a personal level.

During my interim ministry God opened my heart to the needs of this church. At the same time he helped me realize how a smaller church could minister to our family. Shelley had grown up as a church planter's daughter and had a heart for the smaller church as well as children's ministry. After much prayer, we presented this option to the church: I would remain at the Bible college and assume the preaching, teaching, and counseling responsibilities while Shelley would take on children's ministries and administrative duties.

You're Here, Now What?

As we came on board, we realized the church's leaders and the congregation desired to grow both spiritually and numerically. We spent the first few months listening and getting to know the congregation. Their desire to reach out to the community and minister to young families with children was strong.

We considered the church's current strengths: the congregation was the friendliest that we had found, nearly 40 percent of their income went to missions, they desired to be more effective, and they wanted to bring children (and their families) back to the church.

We added to that last strength immediately; as soon as we arrived on the scene, we increased the number of kids in the Sunday school by 25 percent! Not bad for one week's work.

We thought it might be helpful to get an outsider's view, so we asked a couple from another church to worship with us as visitors and share their first impressions. Their comments were honest and brutal. They pointed to the warmth and heart of the congregation, but found the facilities terribly outdated and uninviting.

The leaders of the congregation met regularly to study a book written to show churches how to reach out to their communities. This study was then offered as an adult Sunday school elective. In addition, we planned a Vision Night to listen to the congregation's dreams and concerns.

There was a strong undercurrent among the members to bring back children and young families that had left in search of children's ministries in larger churches. We recognized, however, that by bringing children back into the picture, it meant more than just looking at children's ministries. Most kids don't walk through the doors by themselves, so we evaluated our entire ministry to see if we could meet needs across the board.

Our vision and direction are still materializing. We communicate openly and hold annual discussions (Vision Night and Town Hall Meetings) to help focus our ministries for the coming year.

Our church leaders worked hard and took strong stands that at times brought a great deal of criticism. After the results from our first Vision Night, we began by updating our facility. We developed outreach programs with an emphasis on children. We took seriously the first impressions given to us by our friends and made the changes. The church rallied around these new ministry opportunities. Seeing God work gave power to each new outreach. The love this congregation has shown for its own is spilling out into the community.

We followed a multistep strategy as we moved toward change and growth.

(1) Falling in love with the congregation
(2) Getting to know the congregation
(3) Accepting the congregation's input regarding change
(4) Educating the congregation
(5) Empowering the congregation for ministry
(6) Listening to resistance and responding to it
(7) Weathering the resistance and earning the respect to continue

What Do You Do for Kids?

Having been involved in children's ministry at previous churches, it was difficult at Marion to hold back when we first arrived. We had many ideas and solutions to offer. What we knew, however, was that the best thing to do for a while was to observe. For the first month or so, we looked at what the church did well—excellent Sunday school classes, dedicated teachers, and a true love for children. We also noted what was lacking—no staffed nursery, outdated and cluttered classrooms, unsafe equipment, and no future plan for children's ministry. After observing, it was time to ask questions:

"Can we clean out the classroom cabinets?"

"How about painting the nursery?"

"Do we have to recycle VBS material this year?"

Then we rolled up our sleeves and began to work. Since Shelley was in the nursery for the first month with our baby, she spent her time cleaning and organizing. During that time, she carried home each week a bag of items that were outdated, unsafe, or unnecessary for the nursery. We carried out our work slowly. Although there was a need to make changes, it was best to make thoughtful changes and not steamroll the congregation.

Once classrooms were in order, we worked with the teachers. Most of them knew their own schedule of who taught and when—but *we* didn't! We started quarterly teachers' breakfast meetings before the Sunday school hour. These meetings helped us get to know each other, establish needs, and create a forum where discussing future changes wasn't threatening. (A word to the wise: a cinnamon roll makes everything go better!)

Two foundational aspects of our ministry were in order: teachers and facilities. Now it was time for bigger changes. The main area nagging at us was the lack of policies and procedures. Shelley reworked a manual from a previous church and presented this to our teachers and discussed each item. Not every item in the manual applied to our current situation, but with future growth these policies soon would seem more practical. We've learned that it's never too early to set up policies and procedures, even if there's only one child in your program. You won't want to make up the rules as you go along, so start now.

Another big change was the creation of a Wednesday night children's program. The church had no Wednesday night programming when we arrived. We knew this was an important concept to add, but didn't want to overwhelm the church with too many changes at first. We decided on a bimonthly program held on the first and third Wednesdays; a successful ladies' Bible study already met on the second and fourth. The response was great! After five months, we added a family-style dinner before the program. We pulled in area residents (interestingly enough, these were families who were involved somewhere else on Sunday mornings, but became very committed to our Wednesday night program.)

We planned to move to a weekly schedule once we got established. However, we soon realized that this was a successful program *because* it was bimonthly. The city of Rochester is a family-driven community, and many of its families are overextended. We discovered that a well-planned and purposeful program twice a month met the needs of our area better than a weekly program. In fact, the attendance of our children's program rivaled, and often outnumbered, the attendance of our coinciding Wednesday night adult program—and equaled our Sunday morning children's program!

The next area to tackle in the scheme of children's ministry was special events. Special events are a great way to increase your children's ministry. Smaller churches can pull off excellent big programs. The key? Concentrate on one well-planned program a year and don't be afraid to spend money on it. Additional events can be added each year as you gain a following.

One of our greatest strengths in this area has been our annual Community Easter Egg Hunt. The campground next door allows us to use their property with good roadside visibility. We do a mass mailing (five thousand homes) and announce the event on radio and in area newspapers. We hide more than seven thousand eggs filled with candy and prize slips. Afterwards we invite everyone into the church building for homemade snacks while the kids claim their prizes. We then offer invitations to our Easter services and our upcoming VBS. Because we have all of the children register, we have names to add to our database. We follow up with a postcard and invitations to other children's events. It has been successful because we pour time, energy, and heart into it. Members of all ages are involved in the preparation (shut-ins stuff eggs, the youth group hides the eggs, and the kids take pride in passing out invitations). It is now an event unique to our church and community.

Facing Resistance

Because of the age of this established church, much of the resistance we faced began with, "This is the way we usually do it." Since the church has many of the right ingredients for children's ministry (stability, dedication, and a love for children), the obstacles are being overcome. The biggest hurdle has been getting this church to realize they have something to offer to the children in our community—not just to those who typically walk through the door while visiting Grandma.

Once, to emphasize the church's ability to be successful in outreach, we distributed soup cans with altered labels that read "Marion CAN" in bold print. We encouraged our people to place their cans in a prominent location at home or at the office to remind them of the church's potential. We wanted this little church to know it had the capacity to provide something special to the children and families of our community.

Once the church realized they could offer children's outreach opportunities for the community, they became excited. Ours is a church that will rise to the occasion when there's a need; we just needed to present plenty of needs and opportunities to be met!

Children's Ministry and a Large Order of Fries

It would be great if providing a grounded children's ministry program in your church was as easy as going through the drive-through at a fast-food restaurant . . . "I'd like two volunteers, a teacher's training session, and fourteen well-behaved kindergarten students—to go!"

It doesn't work that way though. Even if children's ministry could be pre-packaged, it would still have to be tailored to meet the needs of your church. Every church is unique. As true as that is, though, some things should stay the same. When we were called to minister at the Marion church with its seventy attendees, Shelley had been doing children's ministry at a church of twelve hundred just fifteen minutes away. The churches were vastly different, but several of the children's ministry rules Shelley put in place were identical.

Here are some of the basics of children's ministries for the smaller church.

Nonnegotiable Items

Policies and Procedures

It doesn't matter whether you have one child in programming or a hundred (or a thousand); your children's ministry will flounder if you don't put policies and procedures in place. Things such as promotion dates, sick policies for the nursery, classroom boundaries, restroom guidelines (is a male teacher allowed to help a girl?), volunteer background checks, and more must be established. All of these things should be in written form, approved by your church board, and explained to teachers and parents. Create the boundaries before you need them.

Safety

This requires thinking of worst-case scenarios.

Do you have a fire escape plan (even for one child)?
Do you have a tornado safety plan?
Do you have a security tag system?
Are your volunteers screened?
Are your outlets covered?
Is the nursery up-to-date? (safe, clean toys, standard crib, and so on)
Do you have a pickup plan in place for children after services?

Do not wait for a crisis to arise before you implement plans. (Our last church had a sniper attack plan!)

Budget

Don't delay in establishing a budget for children's ministry. As much as we hate to say it, money is vital to a successful children's ministry. Do you use outdated material because it's too expensive to buy new? Children know when they're being given leftovers. If you value your children and a ministry to them, invest in it. Plan for updated quality curriculum, large events, postcards, postage, snacks, and supplies. This is one investment that will yield great dividends!

Communication

When we came to this small, family church, everyone already knew the ins and outs of what went on. Everyone, that is, except for us! Even if you have only three teachers, don't assume everyone is on the same page and understands what you are trying to accomplish. Overcommunicate if necessary! A postcard format is inexpensive and versatile (birthdays, reminders of when to be in the nursery, meetings, and so on). E-mailing is a great way to send out quick reminders like upcoming meetings and changes in Sunday school times.

Those are the Four Big Rules that stay the same no matter the size of your church. But where can we negotiate when we do children's ministry in a smaller church?

Negotiable Items

Flexibility

It is great to be in a church where we can make changes based on current needs. For example, because we are a church of multigeneration families, it was recently brought to our attention that the older folks missed seeing the younger children in church. Although our task is to create children's programs, we saw the need to be flexible and include our younger members in the adult worship once a month. We are trying to find ways for our children to be a part of the service while we maintain a meaningful worship experience for the adults.

Number of Programs

Some larger churches have multiple Sunday morning services, Sunday evening, Wednesday night, and many special events throughout the week. The smaller church may not be able to pull off all of that, nor does it need to! We have a strong Sunday morning program and have opted for a bimonthly program on Wednesday nights. We could do more, but what we have in place for now is strong and respected. Smaller churches don't need to have programs for the sake of having programs. Plan for what you are able to do and plan for what meets the needs of your congregation and community. Then do it well!

Interpretation of the Law

At the church where Shelley was previously ministering, policies and procedures were meant to be kept, not broken. At the Marion church, though, we soon learned that policies and procedures were vitally important, but could be changed to meet a current need. For example, we are very strong on the two-adult rule, requiring more than one adult in a classroom for safety issues. But what does it do to the classroom environment when there's only one child in a classroom and two adults? The child is intimidated and interaction in inhibited. Therefore, for the time being, we've thrown out the two-adult rule, and we practice other ways to have a safe classroom: we leave the door ajar and plan to have windows installed. The ability to interpret our own laws in the smaller church is a blessing.

You Can Do It!

Where are you? What are your struggles? How can our story apply to you? To begin with, take inventory:

- How many kids do you have now?
- How strong is your volunteer base?
- What unique qualities define your church?
- Is your church leadership ready to make children's ministry a priority?
- Are you ready for the results?

It's hard not to look at First Church of Big in your town and assume you cannot compete with their programs, budget, and magnetism. But remember, each church has something special to offer.

We were particularly impressed the first Christmas at Marion when every child was presented with a goody bag and homemade gifts, courtesy of several church members. Big churches may not offer that type of personal attention and love. And what child doesn't enjoy being treated like that? (And what parent isn't impressed by that?) What can your church offer that is unique and meaningful to kids?

- Handwritten birthday cards?
- Adult attendance at school programs and sporting events?
- Personal phone calls?
- A parents' night out program?
- Knowing by name each child who walks through your door?

Work on a strategy, pray, have faith, and be ready the moment those kids walk (or crawl) through your door.

Many smaller churches cannot support a paid position in children's ministries. That's OK. A lot of the foundational issues we've mentioned were in place before we came along because the church had a love for kids. As long as you can pull together a team of volunteers with a commitment and a vision for the future, children's ministries can make an impact in your church as well.

We often think of the day our daughter asked why we had to come to this puny church. Our hearts hurt for a moment when she posed the question, but we trusted that God would bless our future. Not long after we were called to the Marion church, our daughter was baptized there. Since then, she's been actively inviting friends to church events and sharing her faith. Soon she'll be a part of the youth group and leaving the shelter of children's ministries. It's the same future we desire for all the children we may be privileged to encounter through the outreach ministry of this church.

Ministering to children starts by rocking them in the nursery and singing "Jesus Loves Me." It moves on to teach the books of the Bible, help them learn about their Savior, and lay the foundation for their future walk with Christ. What is your church doing for the children of your church and community? How will God use your church's abilities and uniqueness to reach out to kids?

Remember, God can use even puny churches to do wonders.

CHAPTER NINE

YOUTH MINISTRY—
DISCIPLING THE NEXT GENERATION

DANNY HARROD

DRAIN. IS IT THE PART OF YOUR SINK THAT ELIMINATES UNWANTED WATER, OR IS IT A SMALL TOWN IN WESTERN OREGON? If you said both, you're right! Drain, Oregon, is where I preach. It is where I returned with my family after living as missionaries in Kenya for six years. It's where I've lived for the past eleven years, not only preaching each Sunday, but especially living and breathing youth work with my wife and kids.

Our Community

Drain is one of the small old logging towns in western Oregon. A common joke from our area goes like this: "Why is Oregon so wet? Because it has only one Drain!" Most of the time people roll their eyes and give a halfhearted chuckle. But we keep telling the joke because deep down inside, residents of Drain like the town's odd name and like having a little fun with it. Drain is a place that eleven hundred people call home. It has been a small town since it's founding in 1872, and it will most likely remain a small town because of its geographic and economic limitations.

The town adopted the name Drain because of the railroad that came through the Drain family backyard. There was no town at the time, and the tracks were laid through Charles and Anna Drain's property. The railroad put up a sign with their name, and it has been "the City of Drain" ever since.

Adults who return for high school reunions or to visit family invariably share good memories of this mill town. It was, as they remember it, the ideal place to grow up. At one time, Drain residents boasted of their Drain Black Socks, the national semipro champions of 1957. The town had three large lumber mills working around the clock, a car dealership, and three gas stations. Today it is struggling to fight its way back to the glory days. Livable wages left town with the thriving timber era of the '60s and '70s. Our schools feel the pinch of declining enrollment and the elimination of art and band programs.

Drain sits in a beautiful valley surrounded by hills covered with cascading Douglas fir. The town itself has struggled to move into the future. Summer tourists headed to the coast, an hour drive from Drain, seem to be in a hurry to get through town as quickly as possible these days. They are passing through our little town on their way to play on the large sand dunes near Reedsport, crab at Winchester Bay, or walk the shops and open beaches of the Pacific in Florence. A few might stop if they're hungry or needing gas. Most people keep right on driving, complaining when they have to come nearly to a complete stop in the middle of town.

Our Congregation

State Highway 38 passes through the middle of town and makes a sharp ninety-degree bend. This sharp corner causes drivers to slow to a crawl. As they slow down, they often glance to their right and notice a white, stately old church building with a tall steeple. It is only two blocks off the main highway, but the San Francisco style slope makes the building sit atop the ridge like a queen on her throne. It can be seen from almost any place in town. At night she is lit up by two powerful streetlights, which illuminate her for residents and travelers to see. What is unique about this church, however, is not the historic building dating to 1883. Probably hundreds of buildings like this one exist across America. It's uniqueness lies in her history of outreach to youth over a period of at least fifty years. It's a good story—one worth hearing. Let me do my best to convey to you what I know about how God has used common, ordinary people to keep a youth program alive for five decades. Because of this dedication, young people have been sent out to serve in churches, raise Christian families, and minister overseas.

If you were to move to Drain, you probably wouldn't be able to get a job in town that pays much more than minimum wage. You might have to drive forty-five minutes or an hour to find work. However, there is one thing you could be sure of—there is a youth group in town you could send your kids to. Everybody in town knows about the Drain Church of Christ youth group. There are about a hundred and ten kids who attend the local high school. Thirty to fifty of those kids attend the youth group, depending on the year. This gets some attention! Schoolteachers know about this youth group. Their opinions vary from "The youth group really helps the youth in our town" to "The Church of Christ youth group is like a cult. It has too much influence on our kids."

From my perspective there is one ray of hope in this economically depressed area—a bright spot in this town whose glory days have faded into the shadows. It is one of the reasons I keep serving here, even though I have been offered better-paying jobs. It is the ministry that my wife, Traci, pours herself into every day. It is the youth ministry at our church, which intersects my larger work in the pulpit. It is why we keep our house open to any teenager in town. It is the youth group at the Drain Church of Christ, and it has made for an exciting past eleven years for my wife, our three children, and me.

The people who attend the Drain Church of Christ see and feel it also. They realize their town has many problems, yet they are not despairing. Why? Because they see hope in the eyes of the youth who are a part of the Drain youth group. They believe that Jesus Christ can change the life of any down-and-out kid forever. In fact, for many of them, this is why they are in church today . . . ten, twenty, or thirty years later.

The church has a few retirees who talk about their days in the youth group as if it were yesterday. This congregation doesn't look at the youth program as a new thing, but rather as a ministry they expect to continue. Fifty years ago the youth group was active and vibrant, full of singing, loving, and serving. Today it is still on course, teaching our youth about Jesus, taking them to summer camp, counseling them through parental divorce, helping them with their addictions, urging them into service for the Lord, sending them to Bible college, and walking with them through the joys and trials of life. How does a church sustain a solid youth program for such an extended period of time? What can be learned from a little church with such a big heart for youth?

It's difficult to get information about the youth work prior to World War II. The Christians who would know that history have already passed on to their reward. It appears that the long run of consistent youth outreach began back in the late '40s. These days, our church attendance averages around one hundred eighty with a predominance of young families. Some of them are new in the faith or returning to their childhood faith. To interview them about the church's history takes you back only a few years.

The last couple to lead the youth group did so for thirty-two years. Their names are Ray and Roberta Heaton. I'll tell you more about them later, because they are a huge part of this story. They are the kind of people youth groups need in order to be successful over the long haul. But even they will admit that their work was built on a foundation laid before they came onto the scene. When that foundation was laid is up for debate. We do, however, have a solid consensus that something amazing started in the late '40s with an elder named Sid Moore and his wife Maude.

Six-foot-two and built like a linebacker, Sid got your attention when he walked into a room. He was a timber faller. He could carry a thirty-pound chain saw over one shoulder and two gallon fuel jugs over the other and still outhike any young man up a steep wooded hill. But unlike many of the hard-drinking, coarse-talking men of the woods, Sid was a gentle giant. He was known as a man who loved kids wholeheartedly. He and Maude had their share of children too—eight over a period of twenty20 years. Sid was an elder who loved to preach and teach. He had a heart for two smaller churches in the Smith River and Row River areas who were hard-pressed for preachers, song leaders, and teachers. Week after week Sid loaded up his station wagon with junior high and high school kids from the Drain church and turned them loose on those small, struggling churches. These young folks learned to serve, teach, lead worship, and encourage the weak. The verse "Don't let anyone look down on you because you are young, but set an example for the believers in speech, in life, in love, in faith and in purity" (1 Timothy 4:12) became more than words on a page for these teenagers. These were the early seeds of the Drain youth group. Elder Sid and these young people went to revivals, beach trips, and camps. He encouraged them to serve, and he gave them the inspiration and love to accomplish their work.

Around 1956, Ruby White and her husband Delbert came from Minnesota Bible College to minister in Drain. Ruby had been part of an active youth group when she was growing up in Redwood Falls, Minnesota. She knew firsthand the value of youth work. She was ready to dive in and help Sid and the others with their ministry. Ruby expanded the work and brought vibrancy, enthusiasm, and hugs. As Ruby devoted herself to youth work, Delbert stayed on as a preacher in Drain for more than forty years. When Ray and Roberta Heaton took over the youth group, Ruby started a program for young kids. Youth work, Vacation Bible School, camps, and youth rallies were what Delbert and Ruby did in the same little town year after year for four decades. Delbert passed on a few years ago. I took over the pulpit from which he preached thousands of sermons. We were looking for a ministry in the USA after returning from western Kenya as missionaries. Delbert was ready to retire, and we were asked to consider the position. Some friends of mine, fellow preachers, warned of trouble and predicted I would be in Drain only a few years. "Nobody can follow a man so loved, who has been there so long," they said. But eleven years have gone by, and I have realized that this church has a tradition of longevity. No one will be surprised if my wife and I remain here for another thirty years. After Delbert died, Ruby decided to stay in town and continue to serve in the church. She has become a great support to me. She prays for our ministry and provides snacks for the first through fifth grade youth meetings every Wednesday night. The two young families who lead this group say they couldn't do without her friendly smile and love for the kids. Ruby has taught this age group for at least twenty years, but instead of being stuck in her ways, she is their greatest support. Sid and Maude, Delbert and Ruby, and Ray and Roberta have demonstrated two qualities to which I attribute the success of our youth programs over many years—longevity and the ability to pass the baton and take up an active role in support ministry.

Our Story

The baton was passed from the Heatons to my wife Traci two years ago. The church finally had enough finances available to hire her to work in our youth and family ministries. The elders knew that Ray and Roberta were going to need to slow down. Replacing them, however, wouldn't be easy. Roberta had worked in the home so that she could devote herself almost entirely to youth work. Ray came home each evening after work as an insurance agent and also devoted himself to their ministry, whether that meant going to a ball game, throwing a party, or planning a short-term mission trip. This was their life, and this was why the youth group in Drain had continued to be a strong entity during their thirty-four-year tenure.

The elders moved slowly on the decision to call someone to direct our youth and family ministries. They prayed. They waited. They were concerned about longevity in this ministry. They needed someone who knew the standards. They wanted someone who loved kids and would point them to Jesus Christ—someone who would be there for the kids beyond youth meetings—in their schools, at their games, and in their lives. As always, God was faithful in his perfect timing. One evening one of the elders spoke up. "Wait a minute," he said, "Traci is already opening her heart and her home to the kids; why don't we hire her?" Traci was already leading the junior high youth group, carrying on deep relationships with many of the high school kids, and working part-time at an insurance agency. Her heart was already there.

The only thing Traci, the daughter of Ray and Roberta, has known is a home devoted to youth and youth group events. Her mom and dad had been doing youth work at the church since she was twelve years old. Even when I fell in love with her and asked her to marry me, I didn't realize how much on-the-job training she had received from growing up with parents who lived and breathed youth work. I thought I knew everything already. After all, I was the one with a degree from Boise Bible College. I knew how to give a devotional lesson, play games, and sing songs with the kids—but I didn't know much about loving kids. However, my wife knew about youth ministry from a heritage passed down a river of outreach that flowed years ago from the headwaters of evangelism and service. It was the understanding of a living, breathing youth ministry—not textbook ideas or thoughts from lecture notes.

Building on the foundation already laid, my family and I began a junior high youth group immediately after starting our ministry here in 1994. The high school group was well established, but junior high youth were lumped together with younger kids on youth group nights. Traci suggested we peel off the sixth through eighth grades and start a new group. *Rafiki* was born. We named the group after the Swahili word for "friends" (not after *The Lion King* character). The timing was right for growth. An average of forty-five kids crammed into our living room each Wednesday night. One night we had sixty-four, which was half the middle school. Traci led worship with her guitar, I taught the lessons, and my daughter and other core church kids invited everyone they could. With this combination, we soon found our living room too small. We began stacking our furniture in the back of the living room to make room for more teenagers. They sat on the carpeted floor, standing to jump and clap for worship. The middle school students seemed to love it, packed as they were, because they were together, safe, and loved. It seemed like the biggest event of their week, since in a small town like ours, there isn't much going on during the evenings of the rainy winter months.

Some of the most troubled kids in town started attending. One memorable evening I noticed a few kids, open mouthed and staring out the window. I glanced out to see what was happening, just as one said, "Can you believe they are coming?" These were the ones who needed extra love and extra time. Sometimes you wondered whether it was doing any good, as you would hear of their troubled home life or discipline problems at school. Looking back, we can see that several of these kids fell in love with the Lord, were baptized, grew up, and are now ardently serving Jesus themselves in various ways. It convinced us that no boy or girl is too "bad" to find acceptance and salvation. Rusty and Keethia Emel, a husband and wife team, led the junior high youth group. They have four children of their own—two of them in junior high. Their kids have caught the vision of family ministry. They assisted their parents by inviting kids and being a part of their parents' work. Traci and I mentored this couple for several years while they led the first through fifth grade group, and then we passed the baton to them. The group continues strong with about thirty junior high kids in attendance each Wednesday. Recently they passed the baton to Darren and Kara Dailey and their four children.

Although my wife Traci and I have moved up to ministry with the high school age now, it was mainly within those years of leading *Rafiki* that we learned the foundational aspects of youth ministry for the smaller church. We attempted to learn as much from the high school youth leaders' experiences as possible so we wouldn't have to reinvent the wheel. Our goal was to strengthen our junior high program and graduate a greater number of solid eighth graders into the high school program so that high school could be a time of falling more in love with Jesus and learning what it means to seek after him wholeheartedly. Junior high kids are generally open to trust and building relationships with adults. When they can be linked in a mentoring relationship with church members for worship, workdays, parties, meals after church, and so on, they begin to feel like they are a part of the bigger picture. Although youth ministers are the cornerstone in touching the lives of youth, a unified church who will pray, build, and encourage creates a much stronger program.

Keys to Effective Youth Ministry

Let me share a few thoughts and biblical principles about youth work in the smaller church. The following won't be found alongside the Ten Commandments, but as we attempted to break down our ministry and prayed about what God would have us share, these have risen to the top as key ingredients. I believe they can be applied in some form to every smaller church's youth program.

Longevity. Every church can think long term. Pray for someone to commit to ministry for the long haul. The Drain Church of Christ has had two high school ministry teams over the course of fifty years. My wife and I have been at it only eleven years, and feel we are just getting started. If it needs to be an elder or deacon and his family, then let it start there; but do not think a summer intern from Bible college will turn your program around. All the newest ideas in the world cannot replace a committed heart and the consistency it brings. The smaller church cannot wait around for a paid youth minister if the financial resources are not there. Ray and Roberta never accepted a salary in their thirty-four years of youth ministry. Neither played a guitar. Neither had a Bible college degree (although Ray is a gifted Bible student and teacher). Neither aspired to be youth workers. They didn't become Christians until their mid-twenties. They learned as they went along. Each decade of youth ministry reinforced that this was a God thing. They felt inadequate by credentials, but God's grace was sufficient for the essentials. A powerful, life-giving verse for us in our ministry has been 2 Corinthians 12:9: "My grace is sufficient for you, for my power is made perfect in weakness." Short-term ministries may make a big splash, or even a large wave, but the river of youth ministry will flow first and foremost through the banks of longevity. It takes commitment over a long period of time by people who do not quit when the going gets tough. We tend to think short term in youth work. We look for young people home from college or a young couple newly married without kids to lead our youth programs until they have children. People in such positions can be great helpers and even leaders, but we should not think only along those lines if we desire to build an optimum program. The current generation of young people in our churches has experienced broken homes, divorce, and abandonment. Youth leaders build trust by proving that they are not going anywhere. If this long-term approach seems out of reach for your church, encourage the church leadership to pray for this kind of longevity and communicate this hope to the church family.

Minister Involvement

Since 1950, I am only the third minister to preach at the Drain church. I followed Hubert Prather and Delbert White. Each of us has gone to camps with the kids, attended youth functions, and spent time in the halls of the school during athletic and other events. Leadership of the ministers and the elders is vital. We work in tandem with the other youth leaders. We are a team. We want to move young people from youth group attendance to involvement with a church family. We want to come alongside students and love and support them. We want the kids to come to church on Sunday morning and know they will be loved and accepted by the minister and the church family. This involvement with church leaders and the larger church family can change the way young people live and affect where they go, whom they marry, and how they raise their own families.

Church Family

Generally, the kids who become Christians are those who start attending church and other church functions. They get to know the larger church family. They feel loved and valued. This is an important piece in the ideal youth ministry. The youth group cannot successfully stand alone. Many kids need surrogate dads, moms, and grandparents. Most of the kids in our youth group come from non-Christian homes. They are not receiving encouragement and teaching from their families. Young people who associate with a church family have a greater likelihood of growing and maturing in the Lord. Therefore, at each youth meeting we stress being at church on Sunday. We network to get the kids rides if they are too young to drive. We sometimes call on Saturday nights to remind them about church. Our own personal research shows that a young person who doesn't become involved in the larger church family will eventually stop attending youth group and give up on spiritual growth.

Camps and Bible Colleges

We promote summer camp all year long. My wife and I direct a high school camp week at Grove Christian Service Camp each summer. This year we took twenty-five high school kids with us. They become our core group. Some of them go early to be part of the welcome team—greeting kids and parents, carrying bags, and showing people around. Ray and Roberta drove five hundred miles (one way) each year to attend a Christian camp in Idaho. Our church believes in the life changing experience of spending a full week in worship, Bible study, and Christian fellowship. Camp provides a forum for challenging kids to repent and draw close to Christ, binding them together and building friendships with Christian kids from other towns. A camp that speaks of redemption and salvation and draws the kids into a deeper relationship with God, the youth leaders, and the others in the group can change hearts in a way few other things can.

Since the late 1950s, our congregation has continually had students at Boise Bible College. We support and love other colleges, but we have chosen to direct our kids to this college due to our ongoing relationship with the professors and community. We take as many as possible to their spring Preview, which introduces our youth to campus life, professors, and students. Youth programs can challenge young people to be missionaries, preachers, preachers' wives, youth workers, and worship leaders without losing the vision that every profession can be a ministry and a beautiful calling. The church needs trained leadership. New churches need to be planted in urban settings, new people reached, and Christians encouraged. Who will accomplish this task? New territories need to be opened up in unreached areas of the world. Where will these missionaries come from? Missionaries and ministers eventually retire. Who will replace them? Where will these people come from, if not from our youth groups? Most likely the replacements will be people who have studied at a Bible college, Christian college or university, or seminary. God can use people in every setting, but the broad base of knowledge that comes from the fellowship, mentoring, and leadership training they receive at such institutions can continue building on the foundation set by their youth group and the church. By focusing on encouraging students to attend one specific Bible-based institution, we seem to have a greater percentage of students who take up the challenge of Christian ministry.

Christ-Centered Meetings

Our rules during youth group are few and simple: positive talk only, respect people and their property, and listen to the person talking. In other words, focus on God. The hallmark of a good youth program will be seriousness about Jesus. The kids know their leaders are going to demand that the meeting not be sidetracked by anything. Boy and girl relationships, disagreements, and cliques need to be put aside so we can focus on God. Hand-holding and other displays of affection are kept out of our meeting times. We have only a precious few minutes to meet, and we want to use that time to point kids to Jesus. You may think this sounds harsh, but our kids respond positively to their parameters. We still have fun at our meetings, along with loud, crazy, and meaningful worship and an understandable, hard-hitting teaching time full of God's love. Most often we teach for thirty minutes, challenging the kids' worldviews and explaining Scriptures. We combine the lesson time with relevant worship and provide a time of visiting over food. Those three parts (Bible lesson, worship, and fellowship) have been the mainstay of our youth programs for many years.

Our ministry with the youth in Drain gives us encouragement that any church can have an awesome youth outreach. Even the smaller church, or maybe *especially* the smaller church, can be effective year after year. It is not dependent on money or extraordinarily talented people. As Paul wrote to the Corinthian church, these three remain: faith, hope, and love. Faith, hope, and love, when applied to our youth programs, produce eternal results.

CHAPTER TEN

MULTICULTURAL MINISTRY—
THE GOSPEL FOR EVERYONE

MARCO DIAZ

I N DECEMBER 2000, MY WIFE AND I WERE INVITED TO HOLD AN EVANGELISTIC CAMPAIGN IN CHATTANOOGA, TENNESSEE. At the time I was working as an evangelist for Health Talents International (HTI), a nonprofit organization whose objectives are to promote medical evangelism in developing countries like Guatemala and Nicaragua. I was also the associate minister for Pinares del Norte Iglesia de Cristo in Guatemala City, a congregation of more than three hundred. I met Judy Smith through Health Talents in 1999. She described the plight of the small Iglesia de Cristo in Chattanooga. They needed a minister who understood the culture and unique problems of the Hispanic population of Chattanooga.

I thought about the lost souls of those people, and I wanted to help. I had recently spoken at an evangelistic campaign in El Salvador where more than two thousand people gathered. After traveling all the way from Guatemala to Chattanooga, I was expecting a big crowd at the church. My wife and I were shocked to find only twelve people in attendance. There were only five Hispanic people from Chattanooga and four people visiting from the Dalton, Georgia Iglesia de Cristo. The rest were volunteers from neighboring congregations. We were frustrated by the small crowd, but after visiting the Hispanic community and meeting several Guatemalans, we knew there was a need for someone who understood the unique challenges of these people. In March 2002, my family and I moved to Chattanooga to work with the tiny Hispanic congregation. There were only three Hispanic members of the congregation when we began. Now, thanks to God, we have more than seventy-five members and more than one hundred people in attendance on Sunday mornings. It has become one of the largest congregations of the Iglesia de Cristo in the country.

Our Congregation

Chattanooga is a beautiful city. Its splendor reminds me of my country with its mountains and diversity of attractions such as Rock City and the

Tennessee Aquarium. Throughout the whole country there is rapid growth among the Hispanic population, and Chattanooga is no exception. Since the majority of the Hispanic population is found in the inner city, the first home of the Iglesia de Cristo was in a downtown storefront. The Iglesia de Cristo has moved several times; the congregation currently meets at the Brainerd Church of Christ on Brainerd Road where we share facilities with an English-speaking congregation. Our members come from several different Hispanic countries including Mexico, Guatemala, Honduras, El Salvador, Cuba, Peru, and Colombia. The majority of the people from Guatemala are not well educated; many have never attended school. Some do not speak Spanish, but rather one of the twenty-three different dialects spoken in Guatemala. Approximately half of our congregation is made up of young single laborers, both men and women. The remainder is mostly young families with one to three children. We have more than twenty-five children in Bible classes and an abundance of babies. Members from Brainerd and other neighboring congregations volunteer to teach Bible classes and conduct a children's worship, which allows our Hispanic members to worship. This has been a blessing as the classes are now staffed with excellent, experienced teachers and there is a variety of activities for our children.

My Story

When the apostle Paul was writing his letter to the Christians in Rome, he said, "How, then, can they call on the one they have not believed in? And how can they believe in the one of whom they have not heard? And how can they hear without someone preaching to them?" (Romans 10:14). That was my concern as well, and after seeing people in Chattanooga from Guatemala and other countries, I realized that an evangelist was exactly what these people needed. They needed someone to talk to, someone to trust, and someone who understood their needs.

In 1999 I met Judy Hernandez while she was on a mission trip to Guatemala with HTI. She explained to me the struggles they were facing with the Hispanic church in Chattanooga, and asked me if I wanted to come to Tennessee to preach the gospel. When she asked me, I remembered the words of the prophet Isaiah who said, "Then I heard the voice of the Lord saying, 'Whom shall I send? And who will go for us?' And I said, 'Here, am I. Send me'" (Isaiah 6:8). I believed the Lord was calling me.

Fourteen years ago, while going to the bank to make a large deposit for my company, I was attacked by six men and shot fourteen times. I was two hundred miles from home, but I heard someone saying, "I know him. This is Marco. Take him to the hospital." Even though I was so far from home, the Lord had sent someone to take care of me. I was in a coma for three months and in the hospital for two and a half years. I went through many surgeries, and during this time I spent many hours studying the Bible. I made a promise to the Lord that if he gave me a new life, I would serve him always. I began to tell people in the hospital how God had saved me. Before I left the hospital, I asked my wife to contact a neighbor who was a member of the Church of Christ. He studied with me, and I was baptized after I left the hospital. We began to worship in his home on Sundays and Wednesdays. I decided to go to preaching school in Honduras. I came back to be an associate minister at this same congregation which grew to more than four hundred members.

Even though I was enjoying my work with the congregation and with HTI, I felt like the Lord was calling me. Even though Chattanooga was thousands of miles away, I was sure that our Lord always makes a way even when there seems to be no way. When Jesus invites you to a great banquet, you need to come because everything is ready. So every time I hear the voice of the Lord, I need to go, no matter the circumstances. The Lord does not accept any excuse. As you see, the prophet Isaiah did not give an excuse. He was ready just like Abraham and many other people in the Bible.

Fields Ripe for Harvest

I knew that the fields in Chattanooga were ready, and I also knew that the Lord was opening a great door for effective work. So as soon as we arrived in Chattanooga, we got a map of the city and started reaching out to people. In the vineyard of the Lord there is no time to lose.

The first thing we did was to visit places Hispanic people frequent: Wal-Mart, the laundry, flea markets, gas stations, Mexican stores, and soccer fields. As soon as we approached the people, we realized they were facing enormous problems such as communication and transportation. In my opinion, not speaking the language and lack of transportation are the most common problems of the immigrant. This would be a difficult situation for anyone. I can imagine being in another country with no direction, not being able to communicate, and without transportation. What a terrible situation!

Hands to the Work

When we found out the needs, we started to offer these kinds of services. When Jesus came to this earth, he came to serve. "Just as the Son of Man did not come to be served, but to serve, and to give his life as a ransom for many" (Matthew 20:28). In order to be a good servant for the Lord, we needed to start serving our neighbors first. That was exactly what we did. The Lord blessed us quickly; within six months our attendance was between forty and fifty people. In one year, because of God's goodness, we had seventy in attendance. Let me share with you some of the strategies that helped our multicultural congregation grow.

Put first things first.

Everyone has dreams of success. Some see success as making a lot of money, living comfortably, and retiring early. Of course these are good things. In this case, we dreamed of helping this congregation grow. The Bible says, "Delight yourself in the LORD and he will give you the desires of your heart" (Psalm 37:4).

If you seek the kingdom of God and his righteousness, he will give you the desires of your heart. My family and I used several strategies in order to accomplish our dreams and establish a solid congregation. The following were some of our initial outreach goals: (1) to supply as many needs as possible, (2) to spend time with people, and (3) to create a plan to help them meet their goals.

Our personal goals were: (1) to love God above everything, (2) to be consistent in prayer, (3) to be faithful, (4) to be helpful, (5) to respect one another, (6) to be optimistic, and (7) to love one another.

Meet together often.

Christians in the Hispanic culture like to worship every day if possible (Acts 2:46). In addition, many Hispanic people in the US have different work schedules. Therefore, one of the strategies that will help a multicultural congregation grow is to provide opportunities to worship or meet together as often as possible, and to have home Bible studies for those who cannot come to church because of their jobs.

Most Hispanic people come to this country without relatives, friends, or a place to stay. They have many needs, and they cry out for help. It reminds me of the story in Mark: "When Jesus landed and saw a large crowd, he had compassion on them, because they were like sheep without a shepherd. So he began teaching them many things" (Mark 6:34). Everywhere we look we see sheep without a shepherd; all we have to do is be courageous and start to work.

Serve sacrificially.

When my wife and I began our ministry, we realized our family would have to make many sacrifices in order to accomplish our goals. People began to call late at night for many reasons: transportation to the hospital, problems with the landlord, babies who cried all night, marriage difficulties, and even dogs that barked continually. We began to see the need to meet almost every night. We were serving as taxi drivers, translators, and counselors. There is a lot to do in the Lord's vineyard. One of my favorite songs is "I Want to Be a Worker." The chorus of this great song says, "I will work, I will pray, I will labor every day, in the vineyard of the Lord." So if you want to work for the Lord, welcome to the vineyard of necessity; there is a place waiting for you and for me.

Help each other.

A proverb popular in the Hispanic culture says, "If you help me, I will help you; if you don't help me, I won't help you." In other words, if you as a Christian don't help me, I don't go to church! In order to reach out to the community, we have to seek lost souls. If we don't go to them, they will not come to us. If I want to spend the day sitting on my chair in my office playing with my computer, the church will never grow. So I urge you to start right now and to see the great example in our Lord Jesus when he said, "For the Son of Man came to seek and to save what was lost" (Luke 19:10).

Challenges We Faced

One of the greatest challenges we faced was to win the confidence of the people. We had to be careful to teach them the simple truths of Scripture in ways that did not unnecessarily offend them. We showed them that we were sincere. Many people were taking advantage of them because of the language barrier and transportation needs. I met a Guatemalan lady at the hospital who had been charged $200 for a ride and translation services. People will charge them exorbitant amounts of money for the smallest favor. But I believe that our biggest challenge was not having a permanent place to worship the Lord. This problem is found in almost every Hispanic congregation, and ours was no exception. In the next three years we moved three times trying to find a better, more convenient place to worship. Praise God, we now have a very nice and comfortable building.

What God Has Accomplished

The Iglesia de Cristo moved to the Brainerd Church of Christ building in February 2004. Worship begins on Sundays at 2:15 and ends at 4:15, but the congregation also meets throughout the week during the evenings. On

Sundays, more than one hundred members meet to worship. Children's classes are provided for the more than twenty-five children. The children have several scheduled activities provided by the teachers including Bible stories, puppet shows, singing, snack time, and structured play time. A nursery is provided for infants, and older children have a Bible class. On Mondays, we hold Bible studies in various homes. On Tuesdays, leaders meet to discuss ways to improve services and meet the needs of the congregation. Sometimes we use Tuesday night as a time for outreach to the community. On Wednesdays, we meet with the Brainerd congregation for Bible study. A class is provided in Spanish, and the children go to regular Bible classes. On Thursdays, the congregation meets for a time of fellowship, which includes eating a meal together and reaching out to the community. On Fridays, the young adults meet for Bible study. On Saturdays, the preaching school meets from 2:00 until 5:30. The preaching school has students from all over the tristate area. We are building a very strong leadership; these young men day by day are getting more experience, and some of them are traveling to other communities on Wednesday evenings and Sunday mornings to teach the Word of God. They also are involved in home Bible studies, care groups, and evangelism. In addition, preachers from Chattanooga to Nashville meet once a month to plan activities such as the area-wide family day that we host, ladies' and men's retreats, and other preachers' meetings. During the year we have special fellowships such as our Labor Day cookout and a combined service with an inner-city congregation. Our congregation continues to grow steadily.

I pray every day that the Lord will give us the tools and skills to be able to spread the gospel of Jesus in the surrounding areas and throughout the world. Due to the difficulties of the immigration status of the majority of the Hispanic population, we are training young men for the ministry. We recently graduated twelve of the twenty-seven students in our program. Following their graduation some of them will return home to start building congregations. In addition to this, we would like to have a strong church with elders and deacons and to become a self-supporting, self-governing, and self-propagating congregation. We will continue to teach students through the preaching school. Our goal is to graduate ten to fifteen students each year and send them out to spread the gospel into the whole world.

Look at the Fields

We must be honest with ourselves, open our eyes, and look at the fields. They are ripe for harvest. The Hispanic community is growing rapidly.

According to the US Census in 2000, the Hispanic population in America reached thirty-five million with an anticipated five-year increase of more than forty million. Hispanic communities are filled with people who are hungry and thirsty to hear the Word of God. I encourage every person interested in preaching the gospel to lay aside egotism and discouragement and to use your talents for the Lord. I also encourage every preacher to leave your office, your chair, and your desk, and start to seek for lost souls right now. You will see the blessing of God. The souls will not come to you. You must go to them!

Get every member of your church involved. Create strategies to reach out to your community through English classes, clothing distribution, benevolence, sports, and home Bible studies. Remember that it's better to do the work *with* ten men than to do the work *of* ten. It's always better to work with a team. Jesus never worked alone. He always was with his disciples. Here are some additional strategies that will help a multicultural congregation—and any congregation—grow.

Make a commitment to God.

I have noticed that some preachers, when they get into a difficult situation, forget the promise they made to the Lord. They leave the flock behind and go away to make money working for different companies. Some have forgotten the words of Hebrews 13:5, "Never will I leave you; never will I forsake you."

Be consistent in prayer.

Do you remember the Parable of the Persistent Widow? This poor widow obtained justice from the judge because she was persistent. In order to accomplish our dreams, we need to be persistent in prayer to God as well. Jesus Christ himself taught us how to pray. He dedicated himself to prayer throughout his ministry.

Be faithful.

How touching and encouraging it is to see ministers deeply involved and faithful in their ministries. In fact, it's one of the requirements the Lord demands. The apostle Paul said to the believers in Galatia, "I have been crucified with Christ and I no longer live, but Christ lives in me" (Galatians 2:20). In other words, if we have been crucified with Christ, we need to remain faithful to him.

Be helpful.

This is one of the big challenges in this country. People like to be served and not to serve. People with needs are just around the corner. If we really want to serve, we must respond to people's needs.

God Is Faithful

Before I left Guatemala, some of the members of our congregation told me not to go to the United States because they had heard that congregations here never grow very much. Many preachers and supporting congregations get discouraged because the congregations continue to struggle even after several years of work. We are so thankful that God has blessed our congregation with rapid growth. Even through all of the struggles, God has remained faithful and provided us with good facilities, good teachers, and hard-working members. God has used me to help this congregation, but our members work as a team to accomplish our goals.

CHAPTER ELEVEN

WORKING WITH VOLUNTEERS—
ENLISTING, EQUIPPING, ENCOURAGING

JERRY STEPHENSON

L OCATED IN NORTH-CENTRAL KENTUCKY ON THE BANKS OF THE OHIO RIVER, LOUISVILLE IS THE LARGEST CITY IN THE STATE AND THE SIXTEENTH LARGEST CITY IN THE US. The city is known for its museums and historical homes. Its arts community has gained international acclaim. Louisville is one of only nine US cities with a professional opera, ballet, theater, orchestra, and children's theater. Louisville's family-friendly attractions include the Belle of Louisville, Six Flags Kentucky Kingdom, Churchill Downs, the Kentucky Derby Museum, the Louisville Slugger Museum, and the Louisville Bats.

This is where the Midwest Church of Christ serves the kingdom of God.

Midwest Church of Christ

The Midwest Church of Christ, a congregation of three hundred, is a congregation of vision and has served the Louisville area since 1920. Located at 2115 Garland Avenue since 1960, Midwest continues to be a vital influence in the inner city, particularly West Louisville, through community-related ministries supported by the church. Midwest's family life and development center, which consist of three large interconnected multipurpose rooms and a large gym and activity center, has allowed us to expand our ability to serve our community.

Midwest is "an inner-city church with a worldwide mission." We're committed to helping our community face and meet the challenges of the twenty-first century.

The Midwest Story

The June 18, 2005 issue of the Louisville *Courier-Journal* featured the Midwest Church of Christ in its weekend religious news section. The article carried the headline "Staying in City Kept Church in Mission Fields" and the subtitle "Faith in Action." The article described how Midwest enlists

111

more than one hundred volunteers from the Midwest congregation and eight other local churches to support various community outreach ministries and programs that include:

A regional jail and prison ministry, where more than fifteen volunteers work weekly with more than one hundred men and women in prisons and jails. Working with chaplains in the Jefferson County Correction Facility and Shelby County jails in Kentucky and the Clark County, Indiana jail, volunteers go into these facilities teaching our New Life Behavioral Ministries curriculum, helping men and women acquire life skills from a foundation of biblical principles.

A drug, alcohol, and jail recovery ministry that provides a transitional home for up to nine male residents at a time. This ministry helps men rebuild their lives and lasts for six months to a year. The program helps with employment search, offers assistance in meeting probation and parole responsibilities, helps the residents meet their family obligations, and supports their efforts to secure independent living arrangements.

A food and clothing ministry coordinated with the Dare to Care National Food Bank currently serves more than ten families weekly.

An inner-city summer day camp that serves up to fifty children in grades K–6. The camp provides working poor and economically depressed parents with a safe and wholesome environment for their children during the day. The camp offers educational, cultural, social, and religious training to children daily, along with organized Christian athletics. With the support of the private sector and the church, the camp offers rates that help parents live within their family budgets.

A free summer lunch program for all school-aged children in conjunction with the USDA and the local Community Action Agency of Metro Louisville. Seventy-five children are given lunch each day throughout the summer at Midwest. More than fifty volunteers from the church community work in the program over the course of the summer.

A family visitation center program (pilot site) in collaboration with the state of Kentucky serving approximately twenty families weekly. Midwest provides visitation opportunities for parents whose children have been removed from their care. The visits are conducted in a warm and caring environment under the supervision of trained and certified volunteers. These volunteers monitor the visits, and the church submits reports to the Cabinet for Health and Family Services. Currently twenty-six persons have been trained and certified as volunteer monitors.

A health and wellness ministry fair for individuals and families. Held in the spring and fall, the fair provides wellness checkups, testing, and general health information. More than twenty-five regional, local, state, and government agencies and individuals participated in these fairs with more than two hundred people attending.

A Rude Awakening

It was noon on a spring day. Our congregation was excited about going into our neighborhood to conduct a community survey, register children for Bible school, and let the community know we cared. Fifty volunteers came out ready to put on the Christian armor and fight the good fight of faith. We came inside to sing and pray. But when we came out fifteen minutes later, we discovered the automobiles in our parking lot had been broken into, their windows had been smashed, and one auto had been hot-wired and stolen. We were shattered. Several still went on with the project, but many saw this as proof that our neighborhood had changed.

Midwest has always been a congregation that went into the community. Yet this new fear and uncertainty about the neighborhood became our first indication that mobilizing volunteers for such community service was going to get difficult. That summer, and for many years following, the west end of Louisville led the city in crime—murder, violence, auto theft, home burglary, drugs, and teen gang wars. This served as our second indication that recruiting and training volunteers was becoming more challenging. Our third indication came from an increasing lack of participation in church work brought on by our members' lack of availability. This was a great concern and caused us to inventory what our members were doing with their time and resources.

Beginning with Vision

In 1997 our congregation did some heart- and soul-searching. We had talked about the need for a family life center and the need to minister to families and children. But were we to build in the current location, or should we find property away from the area and start over in a stable community where the stigma of the west end would not bring fear to our members?

We started by creating a ten-year vision and development plan. This plan set our direction for the twenty-first century. Little did we know at that time, it also helped hold our congregation together when some members who no longer shared the vision decided to leave. The plan kept the congregation focused on Christ's purpose for us.

In developing this ten-year plan, we first had to define who we were and clarify our values and mission. We began by acknowledging the rich heritage our congregation enjoyed. We honored the great leaders of our past: men like G. P. Bowser, who established this work; the first elders, Field Gains and John Hamilton; the great leadership team of J. Frank McGill, our senior minister and one of the shepherds, along with fellow elders Lindsey Fitzpatrick and C. H. Williams who serves us as elder emeritus. These men laid the foundation for where we are today.

Once we had a firm grasp and appreciation of our heritage, we were able to make the decision that was right for us. We could have been like many other African-American congregations with educated and professional members who made the decision to go to the suburbs. Instead, we chose to face the challenges of maintaining a viable inner-city ministry.

Taking the Necessary Steps

The smaller church today faces many challenges; but they can be met, and the smaller church can make a positive impact in the lives of its members, their children, and the community. In my professional life as a community and social planner, I know that for every community and social organization to grow and become viable to the people it serves, certain steps are required. It does not happen overnight. Likewise, there are steps the smaller church can take to overcome and unleash the great potential that sits within its pews—its gifted and dedicated members.

Step One: Prepare your leaders to grow.

The prophet Hosea said, "My people are destroyed from lack of knowledge" (Hosea 3:6). The writer of Proverbs says, "Where there is no vision, the people perish" (Proverbs 29:18, *KJV*). Before a strong base of volunteers can be recruited and equipped for ministry, the leaders of the church must acquire a passion for church growth. Help your leaders see themselves and others in the church as God's instruments for good in the world. In *The Frog in the Kettle* (Gospel Light, 1997), George Barna explains why many churches are losing members, merging with other smaller congregations, and even closing their doors. This often happens when church leaders put their heads in the sand and turn from the pain families, communities, and members of the body of Christ are facing daily. We must first come to know and understand the world in which we live. Geri Redden, executive director of the National Violence Prevention Project in St. Louis, Missouri, defines the problem institutions—including churches—are having connecting and helping hurting people find healing and growth:

Working with clients who come from a family culture of pain, whether adults or children, requires a real understanding of that pain and it's effects

114

on the individual. Unless there is insight into the client's worldview, the source of the client's belief system, we often miss the mark. We try to rehabilitate a client who has never been "habilitated" and we fail miserably. It is as if the worker and the client are trying to communicate in different languages . . . or from different worlds.

Jesus was the master teacher. He met people where they were and took them where they needed to go. He understood Nicodemus, who didn't need a teacher but needed to be born again. He understood the woman at the well, who didn't need water but needed living water from the fountain of life. He understood the disabled man at the pool of Bethesda, who needed someone to put him into the water so he could be made whole. In attempting to impact this twenty-first century "culture of pain," church leaders today must understand the challenges twenty-first century people face. If you can help your leaders recognize these needs and embrace the vision to meet them, you are well on the way to establishing a strong base of ministry volunteers. God is opening great doors for kingdom growth today—opportunities to minister, to touch the lives of troubled and bewildered families, hurting children, and entire communities. In order for us to meet these challenges, we must ask God for his vision and seek new and creative ways to respond to this culture of pain. Many of the methods that worked ten or twenty years ago simply are not effective in these confounding and complex times in which we live.

We sought God's help, and he gave us the vision to evangelize our communities and increase the knowledge of his Word in the church and the world. This vision motivated us to equip the saints and mobilize them for ministry. We began by restoring a strong fellowship within our Christian community. From there we focused on creating a positive image of our congregation in the community. We wanted to be seen as a strong, firm, Bible-believing community of faith characterized by compassion and love for our neighbors.

Step Two: Instill vision in the hearts of the people.

With our goals clearly in mind, we created a vision statement specifically for our family life and development center. It states:

As the Tabernacle old was the foundation that supplied the link and tie between the family and the tribes of the nation of Israel, the church of our generation is the foundation that supplies the links and ties that restore and hold our families and community together. It is our vision that the church serve as the pillar and ground of the truth for the good of this generation and generations to come.

We expanded our general mission statement to make it more inclusive and focused on evangelism. Our early mission statement read: The Midwest Church of Christ in the spirit of love and unity will: grow spiritually, exalt God in worship, seek the lost, build up each other, and reach out for service to others.

Our revised statement added the following to the original statement.

We will strive to:
- Restore Christian values and principles in the homes and educational institutions of this generation;
- Restore the family as the foundation where individuals and society grow and develop under the laws of God;
- Intervene and address the problems facing our youth;
- Address the wholeness of the lives of Midwest members and our community, including both their physical and spiritual well-being;
- Enhance Christian education through the church and the teaching of God's Word.

Our expanded statement allowed us to create an agenda for action, mobilize our resources, and move toward fulfillment of our goals. We created a sense of ownership with this statement by soliciting the input of our members. This is critical because, in time, some will no longer share the vision. A wise government official from the US Department of Health Education and Welfare once reminded me, "The spoken word flies away, but the written word is here to stay." Churches must develop written goals and plans that will lead them and not leave them when men and women want to change the direction of the church or stall the progress of God's work.

Step Three: Prepare the congregation for twenty-first-century evangelism.

Midwest has averaged nearly twenty-four baptisms a year. Changing times require new approaches for reaching the lost. They also require a renewed commitment to the Great Commission. This is no longer something an evangelism committee or preacher does alone. We worked toward this goal by introducing our congregation to *Finding Them, Keeping Them: Effective*

Strategies for Evangelism and Assimilation in the Local Church by Gary McIntosh and Glen Martin (Broadman & Homan Publishers, 1991). Evangelism had to become a way of life for the church. This study helped us go beyond traditional approaches to evangelism and explore new and creative ways to reach the lost.

With our family life and development center, we have the facilities to reach out to individuals and families, serve as a hub for the community, and offer solutions to the problems many families face. Our annual Family Day is one example of our strategy. It began several years ago with the goal of reaching the neighborhood. About seventy-five people attended the first year. Today more than twenty-five government, community, and educational institutions bring displays to Family Day. Our ministries also have booths and displays where we take names and addresses, enrolling people in Sunday school, Bible correspondence courses, and other youth activities. Family Day allows us to equip the saints to reach the lost without turning them off by the traditional hard-line approach.

One of our deacons, Joe Stephenson, drove to Cincinnati, Ohio, weekly for ten weeks to attend a Fishers of Men evangelism training course. Our elders then requested that he bring this course to Louisville. This is one of the most dynamic, hands-on evangelism training programs I have ever seen. Joe's fire captured the congregation, and more than one hundred members have graduated from this ten-week course. Graduates of this course have conducted more than thirty-five Bible studies and developed Bible interest in more than three hundred people. Today each ministry within Midwest Church of Christ is working to develop Bible interest and Bible classes.

I refer to this process as "evangelism reengineering for the twenty-first century." In order to impact our culture, the church must map out new roads and build new bridges that provide new ways of reaching the lost. Outreach ministries that help our volunteers build relationships with individuals and families open doors for spreading the gospel.

Step Four: Mobilize the talent in the pews.

We don't have sophisticated systems for evaluating our members' talents, interests, and resources, so our leaders came up with our own simple version. We ask our people where they work, what level of education they have attained, what special training and certifications they have received, to what organizations they belong, where they volunteer, and where they give their money. These simple questions help us in two ways: (1) They disclose talents we didn't know existed, and (2) They prevent our members from hiding their talents. This simple action step allowed us to plan and develop ministries built around the talents and interests of our members. They now spend their time and talents right here at Midwest, and God and the church are receiving the glory. I must warn you: this stretched our leadership. It forced us to grow personally and taught us much about patience as we trained volunteers to do Christian work from a spiritual versus a secular perspective. This was a new frontier for many of our members, and we did our best to guide them gently through the process. The reward was worth the commitment.

There is no magic formula for enlisting, equipping, and encouraging volunteers in the smaller church. But there are ways to build on the talents and gifts of the people sitting in the pews.

The local minister and elders must agree to work as a unified leadership team, each respecting the role God has given the other.

The minister can't do this alone. Neither can the elders do it without the minister. The apostle Paul painted this picture in Ephesians 4. Both must be committed to God and his vision. The leadership team must be committed to personal growth and development. Where there is no vision, the people will perish.

The leadership team must transfer God's vision to the hearts and minds of his people.

Start immediately to develop long-term vision and mission statements, along with clearly written goals and plans of action. Without this, the church may lose its focus and direction, or some may no longer hold to the church's vision and derail it from the direction it has decided to go. Use members of the leadership team or bring in an expert to assist in developing this plan. It must be done. Remind the people to honor their past but reach for the future.

Prepare the congregation for the Great Commission and twenty-first-century evangelism.

Explore new and creative ways to connect with the people in your community. Train and equip members to reach out in everyday life events, social and community activities, and in their work and play environments. In the process of evangelism reengineering, each ministry your volunteers carry out becomes a saltshaker from which you sprinkle the salt of God's goodness and love into the hearts of those who need the gospel.

Search out and unleash the talents and resources of the people in your pews.

Consider bringing someone in to help you inventory your congregation, or have your leadership team do the work.

Build strong cooperative relationships with other local churches.

The kingdom of God is much larger than any single congregation, and the needs of our society are far greater than any single congregation can address.

Today nearly two million men and women are imprisoned in local, state, and federal jails and prisons in America—60 percent are there because of probation or parole violations. Approximately 4.6 million people are on probation and parole in America—90 percent are in this situation because of drug and alcohol addictions.

The fields are white to harvest waiting for the people of God to come and reap the souls of those men and women who are calling for help from behind bars.

We have more than fifteen volunteers working in regional jail and prison ministries and another fifty working in drug and alcohol recovery ministries. These volunteers represent not only the Midwest congregation, but also a collaboration of congregations in our area. Twelve volunteers from five congregations conducted one recent prison ministry event. Another ministry, the Home of New Beginnings, is also a collaborative effort of several congregations and individuals.

This is a snapshot of how we have reached out to our communities in Metro Louisville, Kentucky. Where will we go from here? We will start all over again, revising our vision plan for the next ten to twenty years, honoring our past and building on our future. In order for our congregation to continue its vital impact upon our community, nation, and world, we will: (1) Create a new vision for improving the conversion of those we bring to Christ. We are finding them; we must now work to keep them, and (2) Create a new vision for improving our Christian education ministry. Our Sunday and midweek Bible schools must reach a new generation of children and youth. Training and equipping teachers and parents as a team is a must. More than 60 percent of inner-city black youth are incapable of reading at a fourth-grade level. Moral training is lacking in the home and in our public schools. We must confront and attack these problems head-on. New visions, a revised mission, and loving and committed hearts will take us there.

No doubt many churches are reaching their communities with greater effectiveness, more resources, and more sophisticated methods. We're simply allowing God to use what we have in our hands. May our God, who is rich in mercy, grant you his vision for your church.

CHAPTER TWELVE

HELPING THE HURTING—
MEETING NEEDS THROUGH RECOVERY MINISTRY

KERRY DECKER

A N EMERGENCY PHONE CALL INTERRUPTED MY EVENING APPOINTMENT AT THE CHURCH. "Pastor Kerry," the desperate but familiar drunken voice began, "I want you to come and cut down the rope in my garage that I'm going to hang myself with." I knew this wasn't a joke. So I abruptly excused myself from my appointment and rushed to Mike's house.

Mike's Story

Mike lived in an old, ramshackle home along a busy street in suburban Riverside, California. Riverside, a Southern California city of about two hundred seventy thousand people and designated in 2005 as one of America's most livable cities, has plenty of nice neighborhoods. Our church is in one of them. Of the households in our zip code, more than 26 percent earn seventy-five thousand dollars annually. Mike, however, was among the 18 percent who earned twenty-five thousand dollars or less. A wobbly chain-link fence flanked his white clapboard house and weed-infested yard. Inside, dishes encrusted with food spilled over the sink and onto the countertops. Out back, alongside the gravel driveway leading to a one-car detached garage, was a huge mound of empty beer cans. Getting drunk was about all Mike had been doing since his wife left him.

Mike's wife found a man online and began a long-distance relationship with him. One day she told Mike she wanted to visit her mother in North Carolina. He gave her all the money he had in the bank and sent her and the kids off in the family car. He thought they might enjoy some time away. After discovering the truth behind his wife's ruse, Mike started binging. Now it had come to this.

The half-inch-thick black nylon rope hung in the dark garage and was tightly secured to the garage door hinge. It wrapped around a beam and was held in place with bent 16-penny nails. A flimsy kitchen chair stood underneath. When I arrived, I took a serrated knife from the kitchen countertop and cut the rope.

Mike eventually ended up in ETS (Emergency Treatment Services), the county clearinghouse for the emotionally and mentally disturbed. From there he was placed in a dual-diagnose, in-patient treatment program where clients receive help for substance abuse and mental health issues. After the mandatory thirty days with no outside contact, Mike was allowed to attend church services and our recovery meetings. Before I continue with Mike's story, however, I want to say a little about the genesis of these recovery meetings.

Wanting More

These meetings grew out of my personal dissatisfaction with my life and ministry. After nearly thirty years of serving two smaller congregations, I was dissatisfied with my smaller church experience and lack of effectiveness in reaching the lost. I've always had a heart for evangelism. And though our church along a scenic tree- and flower-lined parkway had proven to be somewhat effective at recycling the saved, reaching the lost was another story. We stand in the shadows of one of America's largest churches—Greg Laurie's Harvest Christian Fellowship—so we catch the overflow of people seeking a smaller church experience. But frankly, recycling church members never got my ministry juices flowing. I wanted more.

Furthermore, I was dissatisfied with the lack of impact we were making in the lives of our church members. Sure, we had been there, for the most part, when they needed us. Many had grown in their Bible knowledge. Many had forged meaningful friendships. But too many had stalled out when it came to deep inner transformation. Too many were overwhelmed with life. Too many were falling through the cracks. The excitement of their first love for Christ was fading. Something was happening to me as a minister too. I felt too comfortable. I didn't want to spend the rest of my days as a keeper of the aquarium. I wanted to be fishing for men. I wanted more.

I wanted more than the revolving door of pastoral counseling—different faces but the same old problems along with the same old unimpressive results. Broken lives remained substantially unchanged. I was left longing to see families healed and individuals transformed.

I wanted more for myself too. I had grown dissatisfied with routine ministry and my experience of Christianity. Something was missing, and the typical fare of home Bible studies, worship services, Sunday school classes, and pastoral counseling wasn't doing the trick. Where was the hard-core evangelism? Where was the radical personal transformation? Where were the power of the gospel and the move of the Holy Spirit? I began searching and decided to take a closer look at recovery ministry. I liked what I saw. I had no idea of the astounding changes this ministry would bring to people's lives, including my own. But before I tell that story, let me say a little more about Mike's.

Changing Lives

Mike started coming to our meetings. He then told Freddie, an addict and alcoholic who for nine years had been living under a bridge in the Santa Ana River bottom. Freddie started coming to our meetings too. Then David, an intelligent and affable heroin addict, started coming. Soon things began snowballing. Dozens upon dozens of men and women from the community and local treatment programs began attending our groups. Even our own church members were admitting to secret struggles with drugs, alcohol abuse, and sexual sins. People were finding sobriety. Lives were changing. People others had given up on were changing. God was bringing beauty from ashes. Unbelievers began surrendering their lives to Christ. Families were being healed. And people were growing like I had never seen in all my years of ministry. This is why I became a minister—not to orchestrate highly polished worship services on Sundays but to help change lives radically for Jesus. And the changes we were seeing were nothing short of miraculous. For me, the missing link to a power-filled ministry was found in recovery.

I have to confess, I don't like the word *recovery*. I'll tell you why after you take this short quiz.

Which of the following persons needs recovery the most?

(A) The decent Christian.

(B) The Christian who's living a secret life of wrongdoing.

(C) The substance-abusing unbeliever.

Got your answer? Good. Hold that thought for a moment, while I tell you why I don't like the word *recovery*. The word *recovery* sounds too much like it's meant for *those* people—drug addicts, alcoholics, and sex perverts. Decent Christians like you and me think it's the last thing in the world we need. I guess that gives you a pretty good clue as to what my answer to the question is. I think the person who needs recovery most is the decent Christian. I feel so strongly about this that I would suggest that unless you agree, you shouldn't waste your time starting a recovery ministry at your church.

We Need Recovery!

In an attempt to make my case, I will outline some of the practical and biblical reasons I think decent Christians like us need recovery the most. I'll explain why this is the real key to building a successful recovery ministry at your church. Then I'll end with some action steps and advice to guide your efforts.

Let's begin with three practical reasons why a recovery ministry at your church requires the involvement of decent Christians. First, it's a matter of culture building. When you think of the word *recovery,* substitute the idea of "life-changing spiritual transformation," and you begin to get the idea of what recovery is about. Life-changing spiritual transformation is, I think, the culture most of us really want to cultivate within our churches. But to create this culture, we must disabuse ourselves of the notion that there is one path for drunks and addicts to travel and a separate one for the rest of us. The route to life-changing spiritual transformation is truly one-size-fits-all regardless of your hang-ups—even if you think you don't have any, which is the most dangerous hang-up of all.

Second, to achieve program stability, participation by decent Christians is a must. Most churches may not have a steady influx of addicts, alcoholics, and sexually broken persons to sustain a viable recovery ministry, particularly in the beginning. Salting the ministry with decent Christians can help sustain ministry viability.

The third practical reason involves modeling desired outcomes. Let's face it: churches typically aren't regarded as places where broken people can feel safe and welcome. Unless and until the decent church folks own up to their struggles and admit that they need help too, people with more shameful secrets aren't going to push to the head of the line to deal with their problems. You can't be content to sit on the bench and tell others how to play the game. You have to suit up and step onto the field yourself. That includes ministers and church leaders too. The level at which you're willing to risk exposure is the level to which others will dare to go. Addicts are experts at sniffing out phonies. If they get even the slightest hint that you're holding part of yourself back or looking down on them, they'll avoid your church like the plague. Decent Christians set the tone for the recovery ministry in your church.

There's an even bigger reason for decent Christians to get involved in recovery. They need it desperately. I'm convinced that decency is the biggest threat to true spirituality and ministry effectiveness in today's church. Why? Because Jesus says so.

In the Parable of the Pharisee and the Tax Collector, Jesus warns us about the subtle but serious threat of decency:

> "Two men went up to the temple to pray, one a Pharisee and the other a
> tax collector. The Pharisee stood up and prayed about himself: 'God, I thank

you that I am not like other men—robbers, evildoers, adulterers—or even like this tax collector. I fast twice a week and give a tenth of all I get.' But the tax collector stood at a distance. He would not even look up to heaven, but beat his breast and said, 'God, have mercy on me, a sinner'" (Luke 18:10-13).

The Pharisee was a decent man who took his religion seriously. He was one of the religious conservatives and Bible believers of Jesus' day. Transport him from the temple in Jerusalem to almost any Christian church today, and he would feel right at home. He may fit in as an elder or treasurer. He could serve as a minister or deacon. You might find him leading a home Bible study, Sunday school class, or men's fellowship group. He would be the one to organize and lead the church's outreach campaign or some other significant ministry. He would blend right into most churches without any trouble. He would be a prized transfer.

You wouldn't have to guess where he stood on the issues of the day. He wouldn't be afraid to denounce the people who have contributed to the ills of society. Back then it was tax collectors. Today it's drug addicts, alcoholics, and sex perverts. He's filled with indignation and isn't beguiled by soft-headed tolerance. But at the end of Jesus' story, this decent man is not the one who goes home justified before God. It's the man who humbly cries out to God for mercy.

My Story

Decent Christians can easily lose sight of how desperately they need God's mercy. I know, for after my conversion, I became one of the decent ones. When I became a Christian, I jumped in with both feet. I prayed regularly, studied constantly, and witnessed incessantly. I shot through Bible college and entered the full-time ministry at age twenty-two. I preached faithfully and attended as many church growth conferences, Bible lectureships, Christian conventions, and soul-winning workshops as I could afford on my meager minister's salary. I earned a graduate degree. I remained scrupulously faithful to my wife and my ministerial calling.

Yet none of this helped me with the shame caused by the obsessive blasphemous thoughts that have plagued me since the earliest days of my conversion. I have a type of OCD (obsessive-compulsive disorder) and am plagued by unwanted thoughts. They have been unrelenting throughout my Christian life. Nothing brought me peace or healing until I disclosed my struggle to a group of men recovering from their own shameful struggles. And to that group I have confessed other sins that plague my decent soul, including ministerial envy, pride, lust, fear, resentment, anger toward God, doubt, and more.

Decent people are broken people just like addicts, alcoholics, and sexually broken persons. We may have different symptoms, but we share the same disease—sin. The only difference between them and us is that we're better at hiding our shame. That's why the obviously broken stay away from us. We make them feel inferior. Decent Christians may inadvertently end up thinking like the misguided Pharisee who prayed, "God, I thank you that I am not like other men." Instead, we must realize that we are just like other men.   Embracing this reality is the key to an effective recovery ministry. We desperately need God's mercy and grace. We desperately need inner healing. We desperately need transparency. We desperately need community. We desperately need to grieve our losses and forgive our hurts. And we desperately need to open up our hearts so that lost and hopeless sinners can look deep inside and see that we're no different than they are. If decent Christians won't take this risk, the church deserves to be ignored.

Do we have anything to offer a world lost in sin other than our judgment and condemnation? They aren't interested in that. No wonder they've quit listening to us. Or will we be like the one who came to save the world and not condemn it (John 3:17)? That means decent Christians must step out from behind our masks of decency and embrace our need for recovery—for deep, ongoing, life-changing spiritual transformation.

The real question is this: will the people and leaders of your church be known as friends of the friend of tax collectors and sinners? Will you dare act like it? Any vibrant recovery ministry starts with repentance. And the sin Christians must forsake is decency. Once we sincerely pray the "God, have mercy on me, a sinner" prayer and cherish his amazing grace toward the desperate condition of our still fallen souls, then we'll be able to entice others with God's extravagant love. But not until then.

Where Do You Start?

So how do you start and sustain a ministry like this? I don't think it's that complicated. We use a Christ-centered twelve-step program based on the Beatitudes. It's called Celebrate Recovery (www.celebraterecovery.com). The leader's guide spells out everything you need to get started.

We adapted the program to our smaller church setting and keep it simple by sticking to the recommended plan. We don't assume we're smarter than the experts. Could other approaches be as successful? Sure. But I think any proven approach is not as important as the attitude of your church and its leaders toward recovery. You must humbly acknowledge your need for deep, ongoing, life-changing transformation.

Other helpful resources include J. Keith Miller's *A Hunger for Healing* (Harper, 1991) and *The Twelve Steps: A Spiritual Journey* (RPI Publishing, 1994). Miller also has a great video series by the same title that's worth watching, although it's a little dated and the production values aren't that great. Henry Cloud and John Townsend's *How People Grow* (Zondervan, 2001) is worth reading, if you're looking for a scriptural and theoretical treatment of the topic, although they aren't talking about recovery ministry per se.

Successful Recovery

Here are ten tips to help your recovery ministry succeed.

Pray.

Pray that God will send broken people your way. Pray for every aspect of this ministry. Pray for yourself that you may reflect the right spirit.

Build bridges instead of walls.

Recognize the work nonprofit secular treatment centers and government agencies are doing in your community to help the addicted. Be humble enough to realize that God sometimes doesn't wait for the church to mobilize. People need help immediately. And he'll deliver whatever help he can through whatever means possible. Get your name known in recovery circles as an ally in the fight against this incredibly destructive evil that's ruining people's lives and families.

Secure pastoral and church leadership support.

Frankly, I don't give any recovery ministry much hope for success unless the preacher understands what recovery is about and supports the work wholeheartedly. Ideally, he should work the program as a man, not as a church leader. It'll be good for his decent soul.

Get used to giving grace, but don't be suckered by people.

At times I'm a little uncomfortable listening to people share where they really are on the road to recovery. I would rather believe my tidy little fantasies about how spiritual the people are who come to my church. But that's not reality. I can either minister to people's real needs or retreat into fantasies.

To minister to people's real needs, I have to care less about where people are than in what direction they're heading. I need to extend more grace than I may be comfortable giving. And I must keep my eyes wide open and trust my instincts. When I think people are working me to protect some evil or unhealthy agenda, I must go with my gut and take action. I cannot afford to fear their anger or believe their lies and excuses.

Protect the integrity of the ministry.

Be vigilant about gossip and take appropriate action immediately. You can't have a meaningful recovery ministry in a relationally unsafe environment. Furthermore, watch out for creeping decency. Once people start growing, it's tempting to turn your recovery meetings into a club for decent people. Keep practicing rigorous honesty. You've got other messes in your life that the Lord still needs to clean up. Earnestly pray for more broken people to join your ranks.

Put up with smokers on the premises.

I wish people came to us with all their nasty habits in check. But they don't. So we let people smoke openly on church property in an area outside the building, even on Sunday mornings. Temperate Southern California weather permits this. If you live in colder climates, you're just going to have to figure out how you're going to deal with this. I may be too idealistic, but I think changed lives are more important than clean-smelling classrooms. I hate the smell of smoke, but I love the thrill of people in recovery.

Keep it Christ-centered.

Recovery takes people down a path of remarkable transformation. And though the twelve steps are wonderfully wise, the glory of spiritual transformation belongs solely to Christ, not a program, church leader, or ministry. Keep the spotlight where it belongs.

Resist becoming a recovery Pharisee.

OK, I'll admit it. I made some mistakes when I first started out with this ministry. Nobody, especially decent church folks, likes being painted into a corner about needing recovery. I did some pretty good painting. Resist that temptation. Then, once people understand what recovery is all about, warn them not to look down on those who don't quite get it. You still can go to Heaven without participating in a recovery ministry. But you won't have as much fun in the meantime.

Expect resistance.

Some of the hardest moments for me personally came when other church members and leaders expressed their dissatisfaction with our emphasis on recovery. (But if you remind them to think "life-changing spiritual transformation" when they hear the word *recovery*, then what's the beef?) Some people get really, really nervous about transparency. (After all, the fantasies about people's spiritual lives are much more tidy than messy reality. And it's really scary to share secrets, especially for decent Christians.) Others like to take a more theological tack and criticize the twelve steps for not being biblical. (Here's a tip: When someone does this, ask, "Which of the twelve steps do you specifically have a problem with?" Christ-centered twelve steps don't supplant Scripture at all, but they do urge humble obedience to God as much as any good sermon.)

A few may not like the new element (meaning *those* people) coming into the church. All this means is that up to now you've been pretty effective at not ministering to broken people, and you've done a pretty good job of keeping people's illusion of decency in tact. Still, some will leave. That always hurts. But I'm learning to grieve that loss while moving forward.

Celebrate victories and expect heartbreak.

No ministry has brought me more joy than this one. No ministry. I'll never tire of seeing change in people whom society once considered hopeless. I've come to an important realization as a minister. There are basically two types of lost people: those who think they don't need help and those who think there isn't any hope. I've discovered it's easier to convince people there's hope than to convince them they need help. So that's what I'm doing. But not everyone who starts down this path continues on it. David, the affable heroin addict, is back on the streets shooting up dope. Mike, the man who was ready to hang himself, has a serious mental illness and is on medication. As far as I know, he's still sober and drops by church occasionally. Freddie is one of the success stories. It's hard to overstate what a mess he was when he first came to us. And it's hard to overstate what a delight it is to see how far he's come. Just this week, he wrote on his prayer request card: "Praise God! I got work, and I'm enjoying life!" That's so cool.

Situated along a scenic parkway in the birthplace of California's citrus industry stands an attractive but not too flashy church building filled with young families, retired seniors, entrepreneurs, and a mix of white- and blue-collar workers. But if you look a little closer into the faces of the people at Pathway Christian Church, you'll see something else. You'll see living and breathing miracles of God. And I keep praying for more.

CHAPTER THIRTEEN

GETTING ALONG—
FOSTERING UNITY AND HARMONY
IN THE LOCAL CHURCH

GARY PEARSON

WESTMINSTER CHURCH OF CHRIST IS A CHURCH FAMILY OF ONE HUNDRED THIRTY THAT BEGAN IN 1977 AND MOVED IN 2002 INTO A LONG-AWAITED NEW FACILITY ON FIVE ACRES ON THE HIGHWAY BETWEEN WESTMINSTER AND GETTYSBURG, PENNSYLVANIA. The church is led by three elders, Dave Johnson, Mike Justice, and Curtis Wasmer and by minister Gary Pearson. About half of the membership has a background in churches of Christ and Christian churches with the other half having backgrounds in a wide variety of Christian traditions. The church has long had a strong commitment to Christian unity and decided in 1985 to be formally identified with both a capella churches of Christ and instrumental Christian churches and churches of Christ. The church and its leaders have most recently been seeking how best to work with God in order to see more numerical and spiritual growth.

Our Community

Westminster is the county seat of Carroll County, Maryland, a growing county of one hundred sixty-three thousand people in the Baltimore region. Sixty-two percent of the county's workers commute to jobs outside the county, making Carroll a bedroom county to Baltimore and the Washington region. Only about twenty thousand people live inside the city limits of Westminster, but it is the commercial center for another seventy-five thousand people.

Westminster was founded in 1764 while Maryland was still a British colony. The town values its history—especially from the Civil War when a skirmish fought in the middle of town delayed Confederate Jeb Stuart and his cavalry from reaching Gettysburg on time and possibly determined the outcome of the battle and, some think, perhaps of the Civil War itself.

Many families proudly trace their ancestry in the county back many generations, but they are now vastly outnumbered by the tens of thousands of newcomers who, over the last two generations, have transformed a rural county into an increasingly suburban one.

This transformation has caused Carroll to become more affluent. It is now among the one hundred wealthiest counties in the country. One downside is that the ever-more-expensive housing market is making this a difficult area for young adults to live in.

Carroll is the most conservative county in Maryland and is dominated politically by Republicans. The population is about 95 percent white, but there is a small but growing Hispanic presence, especially in Westminster.

When Unity Is Tested

By 1988 I had marked my fifth anniversary with Westminster Church of Christ and was excited about our momentum. Numerical growth seemed to come easily in the '80s and we were moving out of the school where we worshiped and into our first church building. It was a small, unpretentious facility on an obscure street, but it was ours! Finally we could give a culturally acceptable answer to the first question most people asked about our congregation: "Where is your church?"

Underlying the excitement, however, was my growing sense of unease over some increasingly strained relationships. What at first were only a few small, dark clouds on the horizon grew darker and more ominous through 1989 until it became clear that we were headed for a storm that would shake our congregation to its foundation. As a young minister in a church with no elders, it seemed I could do nothing to alter the situation except wait for the storm to strike.

Strike it did in early 1990 when one man (who was perhaps our most conservative member) forged an alliance with another man (who was perhaps our least conservative member), who then asked to meet with me privately. They requested my resignation. Seven people attended that meeting, which set the course for our church for many years to come.

I felt so crushed by that time that I gladly would have moved, but I knew the congregation would suffer and perhaps die if I left the church in the hands of this unlikely leadership. One held extreme doctrinal views that limited God's working in this world almost to the point of deism. The other had once been a popular leader, but his heavy-handed style of leadership and lack of integrity had alienated many in the church.

I refused to resign, and the two men—knowing they would have little support in a congregational meeting—left the church almost immediately. A few other members left because they did not want to be in a church that was experiencing conflict. Another man tried briefly to stir up more problems until he, too, quickly left.

I wondered whether we would recover from this trauma. I thought about staying for another year or two and then leaving with the hope that a new minister would be better able to pick up the pieces. To my surprise, the congregation quickly rallied, put this sad chapter behind us, and looked to the future to see how we could glorify God. To be honest, the congregation recovered much more quickly than I did; but they gave me the support and encouragement that, along with God's healing, allowed me to stay.

Surviving Conflict

Those events happened more than fifteen years ago. My wife Becki and I recently marked our twenty-second anniversary with the church. I am thankful to be able to tell you that that one long episode of church conflict is the only one of its magnitude we have experienced. Conflict has arisen at other times, of course, but never again has it risen to a crisis level.

That does not mean that I have become complacent about unity in the church. To the contrary, while I've healed from the trauma of those events, they are never far from my mind. I have never since taken unity in our church for granted, and I try to be intentional in my ministry to build peace and unity in our church for the long term.

Even when conflict is necessary to move the church forward, I try to manage it in such a way that the result will be a unified congregation. While no simple formula exists to prevent conflict and guarantee unity, I would like to share with you some lessons and insights I've gained in a twenty-two-year ministry with the same congregation.

Occasional conflict is normal in any church and should be accommodated. On the other hand, constant or severe conflict is not normal and may be an indicator that some deeper problem needs addressing. Conflict can be detected in practically every church that received a letter in our New Testament. Rome and Corinth quickly come to mind; but even Philippi, arguably Paul's favorite congregation, was the scene of the famous dispute between Euodia and Syntyche (Philippians 4:2, 3).

We should not have a "the sky is falling" attitude toward conflict. Like all living organisms, churches grow through change. When changes occur, some level of conflict is almost inevitable. Once a visiting church leader came to me with earnest concern—he wanted an explanation as to why we had ended an evening service with a hymn rather than a prayer. Ironically, we have a biblical example of closing a service with a hymn (Matthew 26:30) but none of closing with a prayer!

Churches that rarely experience conflict are often churches in deep trouble. An extreme absence of conflict may indicate an authoritarian leadership that effectively drives away anyone who seriously questions them. Such churches are usually dying. A manageable level of conflict may need to be tolerated (within reasonable limits, of course) as churches work through change and transition. Secure leaders will find ways to manage conflict without feeling threatened by it.

This is the approach our elders took when we spent much of 2004 attempting to discern God's will regarding the public role for women in our worship assemblies. This subject raises strong feelings and convictions, and our elders publicly committed to meet with every member who desired to discuss the changes we were proposing.

Our elders decided to proceed with the changes, but not until the discernment process was completed. Their concern for every member and their willingness to listen patiently to emotional discussions helped us emerge from this transition with a minimum of fallout and membership loss. They provided parameters for conflict. If they had not done so, what was only a low level of conflict easily could have become a crisis.

Unity and Leadership

Unity within the leadership is perhaps the greatest single indicator of unity within a church. Churches of our tradition are usually led formally by elders and informally by a minister. Ideally the elders and minister work closely together as a leadership team. This is our practice at Westminster.

Formal decisions are made by our elders, but they have always welcomed my input on any matter I wish to discuss. Sometimes I have suggested a perspective or shared information that changed their minds. At other times their reasoning has changed my mind. They often tend to show greater patience and faith regarding chronic problem situations than I do.

Congregational leaders must feel free to speak openly and frankly with each other, and even to disagree sharply but lovingly in their private meetings. If a situation is likely to evoke conflict in the church, the leadership should not avoid the matter, but rather process their own internal conflict with each other first so that they will then be able to properly shepherd the congregation when conflict arises within the membership. Sometimes the situation demands that leaders process their disagreements quickly. At other times, and especially with major issues that are not going anywhere, the leadership may be able to take months or even a year or two to come to a consensus.

Once leaders have come to a consensus on a matter, every leader must genuinely support the group decision before the congregation. If any leader is not ready to do this, the leadership needs to continue to process their differences privately until they are all on the same page. A publicly divided leadership can be harmful—even deadly—to unity in the church. On the other hand, few things strengthen a congregation's unity more than leaders who take the lead by vigorously supporting a decision that was not their first choice. Our Westminster leadership is strongly committed to this policy of every leader solidly supporting the group's decision.

Unity and Relationship

The relationships and communication between the church's leaders and members may be the next greatest indicator of congregational unity. While we tend to guard our comfort zones as if they were sacred, it is often the responsibility of a church's leaders to lead the church in uncomfortable directions. Jesus' hearers often found their comfort zones violated by his teaching. His own people tried to throw him off a cliff after he preached to them (Luke 4:29)! We likewise find Paul challenging many a Christian's comfort zone in his letters.

Church leaders today don't have the authority of Jesus or Paul, but we will often need to lead our church in uncomfortable directions if we are to be true to their teachings. We can do so with a minimum of conflict by cultivating close, positive relationships with the members and communicating frequently with them in a variety of ways.

Sustained conflict in the church often signals a congregation's lack of trust in the church's leaders. Churches will willingly, even if ambivalently at first, move in uncomfortable directions only if most of the members have a high degree of trust in their leaders.

Trust is cultivated when leaders invest themselves in close relationships with the members. Not every leader can be close to every member, of course. Ideally, however, every member in a smaller church should have a close and comfortable relationship with at least one of the church's leaders. This may never be true of 100 percent of the membership, but a commitment of the leadership to this policy will bear much good fruit for the long-term unity of the church.

How do leaders cultivate such relationships? The possibilities are endless. Golfers may invite various members at different times to go golfing with them. Leaders who are gifted with hospitality can build trust by having members in their homes. Having a member over for a meal usually results in more closeness and trust than six months of conversation before and after services at the church. Sports fans or music lovers can invite members with similar interests to accompany them to games or concerts. Leaders should find the vehicle for building relationships that works best for them.

What has worked best for me is meeting regularly with a number of our men for lunch or, less often, for dinner. (I keep the latter to a minimum so as not to be absent too often from my own family's meals.) In our early years here, we regularly had other families in our home for a meal. As our family grew larger (six children) and Becki eventually began working outside the home, our ability to entertain guests at home greatly diminished. This is not the ideal, but it is a common reality for many of our leader's families.

My practice of meeting other men in the church for lunch on a regular basis has resulted in my building strong relationships with a number of our men. I am blessed as much or more than they are by these friendships. That alone motivates me to continue this practice. The extra benefits are the satisfaction of helping some of our men find their place in the church and the enjoyment of trust when my preaching infringes on their comfort zones.

As a minister of the gospel of Christ, I am committed to going in my preaching wherever Scripture leads, no matter how uncomfortable it may be for me or the congregation. I primarily preach expository lessons through entire books of the Bible, so I do not skip the hard texts. The strong relationships I have been able to cultivate with most of the members over a period of many years will usually cause them to at least give a fair consideration to my preaching even when it goes against their preferences or what they may have been taught growing up. I learned after a few years of preaching that my preaching will usually be heard by the members through the filter of their relationship with me.

Each of our elders has likewise invested himself in relationships within the congregation. This has enabled us to weather some significant changes with a minimum of conflict. We began, for example, in the late 1990s to have a praise team made up of men and women to lead our singing from the front. While this practice is spreading, it is still by far the exception rather than the rule among a capella Churches of Christ.

A few of our members were quite uncomfortable with this change. We ultimately lost a few members who already had other issues with our direction, and for whom this change was the straw that broke the camel's back. However the majority of those who were uncomfortable with this change stayed on as active and fruitful members because of their trust in the church's leaders. Many of them have since become supportive of our use of the praise team to the point that they now want to make sure that the praise team is leading when they know they will be bringing guests with them!

Preaching and Teaching Unity

A major but often overlooked factor in building unity and minimizing conflict in the church is the content of the teaching and preaching. Biblical principles of unity can and should be taught and preached regularly.

The restoration ideal of restoring apostolic practices and teachings of the New Testament to our churches today is a noble one and should not be abandoned. God's wisdom is far above our own, and we will be blessed when we try earnestly to follow the traditions of Christ's apostles (2 Thessalonians 2:15).

Restorationism also presents, however, potential danger to Christian unity when taken to an unbiblical extreme. The most common form of extreme restorationism is patternism. Patternism is the elevation of one version or understanding of apostolic traditions into a test of fellowship that cuts off those Christians and churches who don't agree with or measure up to the pattern.

Patternism effectively replaces the good news of the death, burial, and resurrection that Paul calls "of first importance" (1 Corinthians 15:3, 4) with the good news of the right church or the church that gets it right. Patternism changes the basis of our right standing with God from Jesus' sacrifice on the cross for us to our ability to correctly follow the right pattern for the church. If patternism is true, then Jesus died in vain. God could have saved us simply by sending us the pattern for the right church.

Members who have strong backgrounds of patternism can create serious threats to the unity of a congregation. This danger is diminished when the church's leaders uphold the true gospel of Jesus, the real "power of God for salvation" (Romans 1:16, *NRSV*).

I have focused on patternism because of its particular threat to congregational unity; but many other aspects of biblical unity should be periodically covered. These would include Jesus' prayer for the unity of all who believe in him (John 17) as well as the multitude of "one another" passages. Romans 14 should be almost as well known to Christians as Acts 2. Finally, the great diversity between Gentile and Jewish Christians that existed in the first century, even while they were "one body" (Ephesians 4:4), is an excellent model for teaching how Christians today can be diverse in a multitude of opinions and practices and yet remain one in Christ.

If asked for my advice on building unity in the church, I would recommend that leaders take specific steps to increase the church's unity and be prepared to engage and manage the times of conflict that inevitably come. Becoming intentional about a matter is often half the battle.

Specific action steps include:

- Adopt a mindset that sees occasional conflict as normal and as a challenge that can be managed and, at times, even used to benefit the church in the long run.
- Manage conflict by leading the process. Provide ample time and opportunities to meet with all concerned members and listen lovingly and carefully to their feelings and thinking.
- Commit to doing whatever it takes to be unified as a leadership team. Let times of frank, private discussion result in all leaders leading positively in the same direction.
- Commit to building strong relationships with church members. Each leader should focus on several individuals.
- Communicate with the congregation often and provide members with opportunities to ask questions and offer input.
- Regularly preach and teach about biblical unity.
- Last, but most importantly, genuinely love the flock and pray for unity.

CHAPTER FOURTEEN

STAYING PUT—
THE BENEFITS OF LONG-TERM LEADERSHIP

TOM CLAIBOURNE

I BEGAN SERVING IN THE LOCATED MINISTRY IN LATE 1979 WITH A SMALLER CONGREGATION THAT HAD BEEN REPRESENTING JESUS CHRIST BETWEEN THE FENCE POSTS OF RURAL SOUTHERN OHIO SINCE 1840. Our services were held in a small building constructed in 1860. The congregation still used outhouses less than ten years before my arrival.

My intention was to drive there each Sunday to preach while completing my graduate studies in Cincinnati. At the end of the eighteen-month period, this good, stable congregation of less than one hundred intended to hire their first full-time minister. I planned to return to Vienna, Austria, where I had spent two summers during college taking the message of Christ into the Communist world. I even sat through a few meetings in which the church leaders examined resumes and listened to sermon recordings from ministerial candidates. I enjoyed that first ministry.

Now, let me tell you about my current ministry. I have the pleasure of serving a strong and vibrant congregation of more than two hundred fifty that uses four buildings to carry out its growing ministries. I preach each Sunday to a more diverse group of people and in a more contemporary worship setting than my 1979 congregation.

The glorious gospel message I preach has not changed. Another thing has not changed: the location of my ministry. Thus far God has given me the privilege of serving my entire located ministry with the wonderful body of believers still known as the Bethlehem Church of Christ, and still situated between the fence posts in our rural community. We celebrated our one hundred sixty-fifth anniversary as a congregation in 2005, just one year after my twenty-fifth anniversary with the church family.

Obviously, a funny thing happened on my way to Europe! I am glad God interfered with my original plans. My long-term relationship with the congregation has played a significant role in the growth we have enjoyed and the harmony we have maintained through seasons of change.

The Need for Long-Term Ministries

One of the key components in unleashing the potential of smaller churches is developing a climate and mindset where long-term ministries can become more commonplace. I am convinced that many smaller congregations could move to the next level—if their preachers would choose to stay with them longer.

In America, the average preacher stays with a congregation for about four years. When we consider that an increasing number of preachers are staying in larger churches for many years, this statistic reveals that countless others are changing ministries quite frequently, therefore bringing down the average length of stay.

It is true that larger, growing congregations are able to provide a more desirable setting for ministry, including greater financial stability; but as long as preachers continue jumping from one smaller church to another, those congregations are not likely to experience much progress.

Thus the tragic cycle is likely to continue, wherein larger churches flourish, blessed by long ministries in several staff positions, while smaller churches struggle as their preachers frequently leave for "greener pastures" in a nearby county or a neighboring state.

Preachers who are willing to break the cycle firmly plant their feet in a setting where they can patiently build a long-term partnership that bears fruit for years to come. Unfortunately, this process is too often brought to a screeching halt by elders and preachers unwilling to make the necessary commitments and sacrifices.

Church growth specialists generally agree that a preacher's most effective years *begin* between his fifth and eighth years with a particular congregation. The implications are obvious. If most ministers are staying four years or less, they are not staying long enough to bring significant progress and results. No wonder so many congregations remain stagnant or decline for years, or even decades.

Our Story

I am thankful our story has been different. When I arrived at Bethlehem in 1979, I was as green as the open fields surrounding our small house of worship. My fear of public speaking was surpassed only by my fear of failure. For more than seven years, I gained valuable life experience as a young, single minister. Several of the church members had been Christians longer than I had been alive. My insecurity kept me from trying to push too rapidly for change.

During those first seven years with the congregation, the numbers remained basically the same. Morning worship attendance fluctuated within the eighty to one hundred range, while following no consistent pattern. An outside observer probably would have described us as a positive and unified church, but basically stagnant. Occasionally I would run into a preacher friend somewhere, and the typical ministerial conversation would ensue:

Friend: "Hey, Tom, how are you?"

Tom: "Fine, how about you?"

Friend: "Where are you at now?" (translation: *"What larger church have you moved on to?"*)

Tom: "I'm still out in the country at Bethlehem."

Friend: "Oh." (disappointed tone, downcast expression)

"You're still there?" (translation: *"When are you going to get a real ministry? You could be doing so much more."*)

I would usually respond with a smile and a comment about my sense of joy and peace about being where God wanted me to be.

Because our years of consistent numerical growth did not begin until after that quiet seven-year period, few outsiders were able to see the growth taking place within the congregation. What happened during those early years?

- I matured in many ways.
- We grew together in unity and teamwork.
- We built strong relationships.
- We created a positive atmosphere in the life of the church.
- We restudied the purpose of the church and began to evaluate things from that perspective.
- We made attitude changes.
- We learned to change things gracefully.
- We gained mutual trust.
- We grew in servanthood and involvement.
- We grew in missions giving and interest.

Were we a growing church? In God's eyes, yes. In most observers' eyes, no. Were those years worthwhile and productive? Absolutely, for without that kind of growth, the numerical growth might never have begun. I have often wondered what might have happened to me or the church had I bailed out when average attendance remained basically the same—and sometimes dropped—between 1979 and 1987.

Because I stayed put and allowed God to work through the relationship we had built, we have enjoyed modest but steady growth for fifteen of the last seventeen years.

We have made several building and parking improvements and completed three building projects, including a large, two-and-a-half level family life center in 2003. I have been joined on staff by another full-time minister and a part-time secretary. Because I have stayed put, the future continues to look bright.

I am convinced God knew I needed Bethlehem, and that they could benefit from a partnership with me. We are a good match. I must also acknowledge, however, that God has simply worked through a preacher who came and stayed put.

Many smaller churches simply need a steady, faithful man of God to make the commitment to come grow along with them.

Why Do Many Preachers Not Stay?

Many preachers make several ministerial changes during their lifetimes. Many different factors are involved in the process. I have noticed several ways that both preachers and congregations contribute to the situation.

Church Factors

Let's face it. Some preachers are given little chance to enjoy a long ministry with some congregations. The varied reasons can be condensed to the following five. Each of these probably deserves a far more thorough treatment than I can give here.

Finances

There are still too many smaller congregations that make very little attempt to understand the basic life needs of the typical ministry family, believing that a preacher must not move beyond the level of scraping by or he will become unspiritual.

Of course, I have known a few materialistic, demanding ministers and others who exercised poor stewardship of finances; but far more simply want to serve effectively and be compensated fairly. Churches should be positive role models for the secular world in how to take care of a good worker financially.

Frustration

Some ministers leave a congregation after months or years of frustration from working alone and seeing little growth in, or cooperation from, most church members. A few even deal with outright opposition from disgruntled members or leaders.

Family Pressures

Like other busy people, ministers do not find it easy to maintain a balance of family life and work. Ministry responsibilities often draw them away from home during evenings and weekends, times when other family members are most available. This is an ongoing frustration for most preachers. Some of them hope that by moving to a new ministry they can change this pattern; but that seldom happens.

Since the ministry is a high-profile position, the preacher's family also finds itself living in the proverbial fishbowl. Pressures and unrealistic expectations are often placed on the minister's wife and children, especially in smaller congregations and communities. Although I have been blessed at Bethlehem not to feel this pressure, I can sympathize with ministry families who constantly face it.

Fire

Some ministers have been burned by the heat of false accusations that undermine their credibility and their ability to minister effectively. Sometimes the fiercest persecution comes from inside the church, rather than outside.

Ministers also deal frequently with unrealistic expectations in helping people. Someone will come to the minister for marriage counseling or for help with a troubled teenager when the situation is nearly beyond repair. Such situations can be difficult for a minister who feels unable to make a difference, especially when a family or group of people suggests that he failed them in their hour of need. A call received from a pulpit search committee in another state may seem quite attractive at such a time.

Firings

Countless ministers have been forced from their ministries because they were fired. Obviously, some preachers may deserve to be graciously relieved of their duties, while others are victims of insensitivity, power struggles, or age discrimination (Note: The subject of age discrimination deserves many pages in another book in this day when too many churches are following the lead of secular, corporate America in this regard.) I am aware of preachers who returned from vacation with their families only to learn that a group of elders had held a secret meeting while they were away. Essentially the minister was then told, "Do not preach this Sunday. Do not pass 'Go', and do not collect $200."

I have noticed that many of these churches are repeat offenders, no matter what preacher is serving in their pulpit.

My simple challenge to church elders and deacons is to be like Jesus, whether times are good or tensions are high. Common courtesy and Christian decency among church leaders could significantly increase the average stay of preaching ministers.

Preacher Factors

Even the most gracious, willing, and stable congregations lose their preachers from time to time. Several personal factors in the minister's life can play a role in the decision to move on. I will focus on seven of them, realizing that this treatment is merely a simplified summary.

Personal exhaustion

This factor is tied to some of the church factors and often results in a preacher leaving vocational ministry altogether, either temporarily or permanently. One key to healthy, long-term ministry is developing a strong devotional life, personal and ministerial accountability, delegation of responsibility, time management, and a balanced personal life.

Personal challenge

Often a preacher reluctantly leaves a ministry he loves because he sees a congregation or type of ministry where he can better use his gifts and impact more people with the gospel. It is hard to fault such decisions when a person is genuinely seeking the best for the kingdom of God, and money and status are irrelevant.

Personal ambition

Even though this type of move may, on the outside, appear similar to the previous factor, it can involve a more self-centered motivation that may have little to do with the will of God. This climbing-the-ladder mentality causes ministers to see smaller churches as mere steppingstones on the pathway to bigger and better things.

Personal sin

Each of our hearts has been broken as we have watched talented, respected men throw away their ministries with careless behavior and foolish choices. Their churches and families usually pay a heavy price for years.

Personal conflict

There will always be differences of opinion, strong disagreements, and various personal issues in congregations and among church leaders, just as there were in Bible times. The church is made up of people who are far from perfect, so conflicts will arise. Occasionally such conflicts and tensions will grow to the point where a minister feels he can no longer be effective in that congregation.

Long-term ministry demands that ministers, elders, and other church members learn to deal with conflict and strained relationships in a timely and biblical way before they reach a crisis point.

Personal and family issues

Sometimes ministers will move on to another place of service because they feel the new setting will benefit their family and health situations, their own aging process, or that of their extended family. Such situations are understandable, but these decisions should also include an honest look at the big picture, the timing, and how both the family and the congregation will be affected.

Personal laziness

Staying in a long-term ministry demands personal growth—a price some ministers are not willing to pay. There is a temptation for preachers who move every three to five years to continue pulling the same sermons and bags of tricks out of their files. Serving year after year with the same people requires creativity, freshness, and constant study—priorities under any circumstance.

My challenge to preachers is to love God, love people, work hard, develop a balanced life, be like Jesus, and remember that the ministry is not about us, our comfort, or our personal desires, but about our eternal God and our faithfulness to the mission Jesus sent us to complete.

I would also like to pass on the advice of Wayne Smith, longtime minister of the Southland Christian Church in Lexington, Kentucky. Wayne advises preachers who are tempted to resign to wait a month before doing anything. Then if they are still convinced they should resign, pray about it for a month. After that time, if they are still sure, write a resignation letter, but wait yet another month before submitting it.

The Blessings of Staying Put

Many blessings come to the congregation and preacher who labor together faithfully in a long, lasting relationship. On two occasions when I was preparing to write or speak about long-term ministry, I surveyed several well-respected ministers who had enjoyed a long ministry with their congregations. I asked them to share what they felt were the greatest blessings. Several of the following responses were repeated by a majority of those surveyed. I concur with each observation.

- Stability—for yourself, your family, and for challenging young people to enter specialized Christian service.
- Establishing roots in the community and the church.
- Accountability.
- Relationships—sharing the hurts, faults, joys and sorrows.
- Seeing growth in number and in spirit from seeds you have put into the ground.
- Baptizing and laboring together with several generations in the same family.
- Earning trust, respect, and appreciation.
- Goal-setting.
- Leading gracefully through change in the church.
- Learning how best to minister in that particular setting.
- Helping develop a spirit of love and unity in which you can comfortably carry out your ministry.
- Helping develop a healthy church reputation in the community.
- The satisfaction of sticking it out through tough times.
- Seeing doors open for ministry, something that often happens slowly.

To this list I would add three more blessings which I have experienced:

- Seeing visible results from your labors in facilities, programming, numbers, and most of all, growth in individual lives.
- Developing a strong bond with foreign missionaries supported by the church.
- Outliving stupid personal mistakes.

These blessings should provide plenty of motivation to strive for a long ministry relationship.

I recently celebrated the twenty-fifth wedding anniversary of the first couple I married at Bethlehem. I have performed weddings for four young ladies whom I held as newborn babies, and have since held one of their newborn babies. We recently ordained a young man as a deacon who was a baby when I came. I taught him at church camp, baptized him into Christ, guided him in youth group, performed his wedding, held his newborn son, and was with him when his father died.

I met a young boy from an area church many years ago, spent time with him at church camps and youth rallies, performed his wedding, and spoke at his ordination to the ministry. He has now returned to the area and serves as our associate minister. Long-term relationships like these are priceless.

The Challenges of Staying Put

Like other aspects of life and ministry, challenges accompany the blessings. I offer the following list of challenges as a helpful warning from my own experience and the observations of other long-term ministers.

- Staying fresh.
- Becoming content, comfortable, and complacent.
- Avoiding the temptation not to take a strong stand in some areas because you and your family are comfortable.
- Maintaining the discipline of personal growth.
- Being taken for granted and taking others for granted.
- Abusing people's trust and the freedom that results from it.
- Thinking you are indispensable.
- Being responsible with the amount of information you know about people in the congregation.
- Seeing faithful, older servants of Christ not being shown respect by relative newcomers.
- Accepting too much personal credit for progress in the church.
- Feeling entitled to certain rewards, privileges, or blessings.
- Being tempted to whine, shine, or recline.
- Preparing the church leaders and the congregation for the challenging transition that often follows a long ministry.

Ignoring some of these warnings can eventually hinder ministry and reverse some of the blessings.

Developing a Healthy View of Ministry

If we intend to honor God with our service, we must develop a healthy view of ministry—not one that is determined by the secular culture around us, our own personal ambitions, or a spirit of competition with other preachers or congregations. A healthy view of ministry will go a long way toward preventing ministries from being cut short.

If we are engaged in ministry, we're engaged in more than an occupation.

- In an occupation we try to move up the ladder. In ministry we try to serve God however he leads.
- In an occupation we tend to focus on our life. In ministry we seek to bring true life to other people's lives.
- In an occupation we want to be noticed. In ministry we want Christ to be noticed.
- In an occupation we tend to compare our work and its results with that of other workers. In ministry we strive to be faithful and serve with excellence no matter what others are doing.

The real point in ministry is faithfulness to our mission for Christ. In Jesus' Parable of the Talents (Matthew 25), he made it clear that each of us is to be faithful with our unique gifts in our unique settings. One man in the parable had been given five talents of money and made five more. Another man doubled the two he was given. It is tempting to conclude that the first man was more successful.

Yet Jesus says both were successful. The commendation given to the man in verse 23 is identical to the commendation given to the man in verse 21. The men were equally faithful and successful. I believe more ministers would stay longer in ministries which are slowly progressing if they didn't feel like they had to measure up to the false idea of success that is often prevalent in ministry circles and conferences.

Many ministers are laboring faithfully in smaller congregations and progressing toward future numerical growth, only to feel a subtle pressure from their preacher friends (and their own self-doubts) to look for what they assume is a more significant ministry.

If you find yourself in the midst of that emotional struggle, I encourage you to seek a broader perspective in the following questions.

At what attendance level does a ministry become significant? One hundred fifty? Two hundred seventy-five? Four hundred? A thousand? Is the faithful preacher who pours his life into a small group of inner-city people less productive than the man preaching to four hundred in the suburbs? Is the courageous missionary struggling deep inside the Muslim world with a handful of converts less productive than the man leading two thousand in a more receptive field?

Was Jesus more productive when he fed the five thousand than when he talked to Nicodemus or the Samaritan woman, or when he discipled the Twelve? When Philip baptized throngs in Samaria (Acts 8), was he more productive than when he converted the one Ethiopian on the desert road?

Remember, you do not have to prove to some well-meaning preacher friend that what you are doing in ministry is significant and productive. We serve the Lord of the universe who calls all kinds of people to all kinds of ministries in all kinds of settings so that all people can have the opportunity to respond to the gospel message of Christ. Jesus is the master we are seeking to please.

Let's not assume God wants us to stay in one location our entire life. But neither should we assume every phone call or church packet from a pulpit search committee (at a larger church, of course) is a clear calling from the Lord.

Let's seek God's glory. Let's humbly discern his will. Let's not give up too soon on people or situations. Let's faithfully serve in God's power which is able to do immeasurably more than all we can ask or imagine.

CHAPTER FIFTEEN

UNLEASHING YOUR POTENTIAL

SHAWN MCMULLEN

YOU'VE HEARD FROM CHURCH LEADERS FROM ACROSS THE COUNTRY. You've looked inside their communities, their churches, and their ministries. You've learned about their vision, their strategies, their struggles, and their victories. You've listened to their advice and considered their actions steps.

So where will you go from here?

Where Growth Comes From

Let's begin by considering this simple principle: Only God can grow a church.

That's how it was on the Day of Pentecost. "And the Lord added to their number daily those who were being saved" (Acts 2:47). That's how Paul saw it. He described Jesus as "the Head, from whom the whole body, supported and held together by its ligaments and sinews, grows as God causes it to grow" (Colossians 2:19). He reminded a group of bickering believers, "I planted the seed, Apollos watered it, but God made it grow. So neither he who plants nor he who waters is anything, but only God, who makes things grow" (1 Corinthians 3:6, 7).

Make no mistake. You and I do not grow the church. That's God's work. We can pray for growth. We can set the stage for growth. We can work for growth. But in the end, God alone grows the church.

In many ways, that's why some churches grow large and some don't. You can factor in the vision of the leaders, the location of the building, the surrounding population, and a hundred other variables. And still it comes down to this. Churches grow because God causes them to grow.

If you're part of a smaller church, I hope you find this principle encouraging. There may be many reasons why your church hasn't experienced explosive growth. In fact, that may not be what God has in mind for your church.

As I began this project, I contacted dozens of Christian leaders across the country, asking them to tell me about smaller churches they knew that were doing great things in ministry. One well-meaning leader of a parachurch organization responded to my query with a caution. "Finding smaller churches that excel in ministry may prove to be a problem," he noted, "because any church that excels in ministry is going to grow and will not remain a smaller church."

I know this brother had good intentions, and he certainly didn't mean to be discouraging. But I disagree with his view of ministry and the local church. In fact, I think this book proves him wrong. You've just read about a number of smaller churches that are doing great things for God's kingdom. Their geographical location, population, and other factors may limit numeric growth, but they're taking what they've been given and glorifying God with it.

I'm glad that in the last few years we've been hearing more about church health and less about church growth. True, healthy churches grow (and church growth is important), but who determines when a church is growing and when it is not? Is it simply a matter of attendance records? Membership rolls? Programs initiated? Or is there more to church growth than meets the eye?

Only God can grow a church. And he alone evaluates growth.

Part of the Big Picture

While we're at it, let's keep this principle in mind too: Your smaller church is an integral part of Christ's body—a valuable asset in God's kingdom.

Don't forget that.

When you focus on an area of ministry and work diligently with your congregation to serve God and your community through that ministry, you—and thousands of others in thousands of churches throughout the world—are helping to accomplish God's purpose on earth.

You're part of the big picture.

I love the magnificent scene John depicts in the book of Revelation of the people and activity surrounding the throne of God in Heaven.

> After this I looked and there before me was a great multitude that no one could count, from every nation, tribe, people and language, standing before the throne and in front of the Lamb. They were wearing white robes and were holding palm branches in their hands. And they cried out in a loud voice: "Salvation belongs to our God, who sits on the throne, and to the Lamb" (Revelation 7:9, 10).

Someday you and I will stand in the presence of God in Heaven, part of a vast, innumerable multitude. I look forward to that day. But until then, I'm part of a vast multitude on earth—a multitude of believers and churches (larger and smaller) living their lives to the glory of God. What the good folks in my smaller church accomplish for the kingdom may not make the headlines, but collectively, with all the other saints and churches around the world, we're doing something huge. We're part of the big picture.

Like a Mighty Army

As you and your church begin to unleash your potential, remember that you are engaged in a spiritual battle. Paul reminds us that "our struggle is not against flesh and blood, but against the rulers, against the authorities, against the powers of this dark world and against the spiritual forces of evil in the heavenly realms" (Ephesians 6:12).

Battles are fought on many fronts. Take the Civil War, for example. Historians recognize three hundred eighty-four principle battles in the War Between the States, but the actual number of armed conflicts during the war (ranging from minor skirmishes to battles) comes closer to ten thousand five hundred.

The spiritual war we are engaged in—a war fought not for political or geographical reasons but for the souls of men, women, and children—is fought on many fronts as well. There is only one war, and thank God its outcome was determined more than 2,000 years ago by the death and resurrection of Jesus Christ. But still the battles of this great war continue to be waged across our nation and around the world.

These battles are being fought daily in our communities, our churches, and our homes. Some battles may get more publicity than others, but each battle is eternally important. *Your* battle is eternally important.

Taking Your Hill

Wherever you live, and wherever your church is located, you are a part of God's great army. Your mission is to take the hill to which you've been assigned—to capture your community for Jesus Christ. As you fulfill your part of the battle plan, you are contributing to the overall war effort. You and the people who serve with you are aiding the growth and expansion of God's kingdom.

Imagine what would happen if every church in every community took its hill for Christ. Imagine how that would change the spiritual landscape of our nation!

Leading the Charge

I hope by now you're feeling confident about the value of your ministry and the ability of your church to positively impact your community for Christ. I also hope you're determined to do your part to help your congregation unleash its potential.

Perhaps you're thinking, *I know this needs to be done, but I'm not a leader. Someone else will have to do that.* You may be right. But then again, you may not be.

God may be looking to you to mobilize your church and help change your community. He may be depending on you to lead the charge. And why wouldn't he? He's taken unlikely people in the past and made leaders out of them.

God made a leader out of a reluctant man named Moses. When God met Moses at Mount Horeb and charged him to bring the Israelites out of Egypt, Moses asked, "Who am I, that I should go?" (Exodus 3:11). God explained that he would go with him, but Moses still balked. "What if they do not believe me or listen to me?" (4:1). God showed Moses his mighty power by turning his staff into a snake and by afflicting his hand with leprosy and then restoring it. Moses knew he was losing ground, but he offered another excuse. "O Lord, I have never been eloquent . . . I am slow of speech and tongue" (4:10). So God promised to help him speak and to teach him what to say. Finally, with no excuses left Moses pleaded, "O Lord, please send someone else to do it" (4:13). It's hard to imagine a more reluctant leader. But God had a job for Moses, and he would not take no for an answer.

God made a leader out of an obscure man named David. Do you remember where David was when the prophet Samuel came to Jesse's house to anoint one of his sons king over Israel? David was the youngest, and the least likely to be anointed king, so Jesse put him outside with the flocks while he paraded his other sons before the prophet. That didn't stop Samuel from singling David out and anointing him, however. Later God reminded David, "I took you from the pasture and from following the flock to be ruler over my people Israel" (2 Samuel 7:8).

God made a leader out of an angry man named Saul. Paul described his pre-conversion days this way: "I too was convinced that I ought to do all that was possible to oppose the name of Jesus of Nazareth. And that is just what I did" (Acts 26:9, 10). It wasn't until Jesus appeared to him on the road to Damascus and gave him his marching orders that Saul realized his error. But once he did, he was transformed from the church's most fierce enemy to one of its most beloved leaders.

Sometimes the people who are the most hesitant to lead make the best leaders. A. W. Tozer wrote,

A true and safe leader is likely to be one who has no desire to lead, but is forced into a position by the inward pressure of the Holy Spirit and the press of [circumstances]. . . . There was hardly a great leader from Paul to the present day but was drafted by the Holy Spirit for the task, and commissioned by the Lord to fill a position he had little heart for.[1]

Does that describe you? You may not think so, but you may be just the person God has in mind to help your church unleash its potential.

Shaping Your Church's Heart

This is a good place to talk about change and how to go about it. In reading this book, you may have come across several ministries you want your church to pursue. Perhaps this book has helped you narrow your focus to a specific area of ministry. Beginning that ministry, however, may call for some adjustments. Certain changes may need to take place, and they may not be widely accepted. How will you handle that?

Let me suggest that you move prayerfully, methodically, graciously, and slowly to achieve your goal—even if it means delaying your plans to make sure as many members as possible are on board before you begin. Take it upon yourself, if necessary, to change the atmosphere in your church. Set an example for the believers by your willingness to accept positive changes others recommend. Get behind new ideas and support those who propose them. Earn trust and respect through your personal holiness, blamelessness, and integrity. Invest yourself in the lives of others.

Take advantage of every opportunity to promote a kingdom consciousness in people's hearts. Show them by word and example how to put God's kingdom above their personal needs and preferences. When church members cultivate a kingdom consciousness, issues like music and worship styles, overcrowding, use of the building, and finances take a back seat to reaching the lost and building up believers.

Keep in mind, however, that such change in heart comes quickly to some and slowly to others. Take your time. Teach patiently. Love extravagantly. Forgive completely. Model consistently. Trust God to honor your sincere, patient, sacrificial, and loving spirit as you help change your church's heart and move people toward more effective ministry.

A Parting Thought

I'm glad you read this book. I pray that God has used it to encourage you in your ministry. And I pray that God uses it to encourage the church you serve.

As I mentioned in the first chapter, I serve a smaller church. Like many other preachers, occasionally I get offers from larger churches to interview for ministry. When that happens, I politely decline the invitation. Why? Because I love the church I serve. I believe God has bigger plans for this smaller congregation, and if he wills, I'd like to be around to see those plans materialize.

I hope you feel the same about the church you serve. Whether you're a preacher, a leader, a teacher, or a ministry volunteer, I hope you can say that you genuinely love the church you serve.

Jesus Christ set the example for us. He "loved the church and gave himself up for her" (Ephesians 5:25). Of all the things that help a church unleash its potential, the love its members have—for Jesus Christ and for one another—is by far the greatest, most powerful, and most effective tool. If you want to unleash the potential of the church you serve, love God and love the people.

I've certainly found that true in my ministry. In fact, I wrote about this love in an editorial I penned for THE LOOKOUT. If you'll indulge me, I'd like to leave you with these thoughts.

Why I Love the Church I Serve

The Call to Ministry

"A great door for effective work has opened to me" (1 Corinthians 16:9).

My work with the church I serve began with a phone call. "Our minister resigned," the voice on the phone explained. "Will you fill the pulpit for us?"

After preaching for several months, I was asked to assume the position permanently. I was reluctant at first. But then I was told, "We know editing THE LOOKOUT is a demanding ministry, but we still want you to be our preacher. Tell us what you have time to do, and we'll do the rest."

I agreed. And the church has been true to its promise. Some of our men are natural shepherds and evangelists. When we plan seminars and revivals, they scour the neighborhoods inviting people to attend. If members become slack in their attendance, these men are the first to place phone calls and make personal visits.

Our folk willingly volunteer to mow the lawn, clean the building, and make needed repairs. Others faithfully teach Sunday school, lead youth worship, prepare Communion, print the Sunday bulletins, and direct Vacation Bible School.

I feel grateful that God called me to a ministry where the workload is willingly and cheerfully shared.

The Privilege of Ministry

"Although I am less than the least of all God's people, this grace was given me: to preach to the Gentiles the unsearchable riches of Christ" (Ephesians 3:8).

I don't feel worthy of the honor, but I love to preach and teach. I cherish the time I spend in God's Word preparing sermons and lessons. I look forward to presenting the fruit of my study every Sunday morning and evening. I'm honored to team up with my father to teach our Wednesday night Bible study. I thrill to see lives changed by the power of the Word.

The People in Ministry

"God can testify how I long for all of you with the affection of Christ Jesus" (Philippians 1:8).

I love the adults in our church. I look forward to the warm, friendly handshakes that greet me when I enter the building. I enjoy seeing the smiles on their faces and hearing their hearty laughter. I admire their desire to learn and grow.

I love the young people in our church. I delight in our brief conversations as they leave the church building on Sunday mornings. "Do you like preschool?" "Did your team win Friday night?" "When will you take your driver's test?" "Have you finished your weekend homework?" (Once a parent, always a parent!)

On Sunday evenings in warm weather, we often gather on our property and hold vespers services around a campfire. We sing and pray and study God's Word. More often than not, we find time to roast hot dogs and marshmallows too. Many stay after the service to extend the fellowship time.

The Joy of Ministry

"What is our hope, our joy, or the crown in which we will glory in the presence of our Lord Jesus when he comes? Is it not you? Indeed, you are our glory and joy" (1 Thessalonians 2:19, 20).

My ministry is a source of great joy to me. I feel joy when I visit in the homes of newly attending families. I feel joy when I baptize parents and their children into Christ. I feel joy when I stop by the home of a young couple to congratulate them on the birth of their first child. And in a subdued way, I feel joy when I preach the funeral of a faithful saint who has gone to be with the Lord.

I feel joy when I lead the congregation in singing "How Great Thou Art" and "When We All Get to Heaven." And I feel joy when I turn off the light in my office on Sunday evenings, take one last walk through the auditorium, and say silently to God as I shut the door behind me, "Thank you, Lord, for this incredible privilege."

That's why I love the church I serve.

May God richly bless your efforts to unleash the potential of the church you love and serve.

[1]A. W. Tozer, *The Reaper*, February 1962, p. 459. Quoted by J. Oswald Sanders in *Spiritual Leadership* (Moody, 1994), pp. 29, 30.

Two New Resources
from Standard Publishing

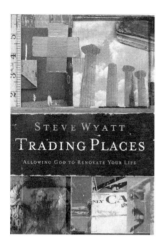

Trading Places
Allowing God to Renovate Your Life
Steve Wyatt

Trading Places examines what it takes to make changes that will last and challenges readers to understand that real-life transformation isn't about external circumstances, but what you allow God to do on the inside.

Second Guessing God
Hanging On When You Can't See His Plan
Brian Jones

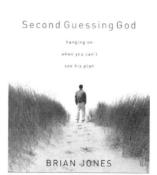

Each year, author Brian Jones invites his congregation to submit questions for a sermon series he calls "Questions I Want to Ask God." One question is always asked more than any other: "Why does God allow bad things to happen?" This book is Jones's response to that question. Like a good friend, Brian comes alongside those seeking help in the trials of life to help them find meaning and strength.

Place your order by calling 1-800-543-1353.